To Troe

With lo..

fr continued success
looking fwd to working
together

Ken Col..
4-25-13

IGNITE

YOUR BUSINESS

TRANSFORM

YOUR WORLD

Published by CelebrityPress™, Orlando, FL
A division of The Celebrity Branding Agency®

Celebrity Branding® is a registered trademark
Printed in the United States of America.

ISBN: 9780982908334
LCCN: 2010936989

This publication is designed to provide accurate and authoritative information with regard to the subject matter covered. It is sold with the understanding that the publisher is not engaged in rendering legal, accounting, or other professional advice. If legal advice or other expert assistance is required, the services of a competent professional should be sought. The opinions expressed by the authors in this book are not endorsed by CelebrityPress™ and are the sole responsibility of the author rendering the opinion.

Most CelebrityPress™ titles are available at special quantity discounts for bulk purchases for sales promotions, premiums, fundraising, and educational use. Special versions or book excerpts can also be created to fit specific needs.

For more information, please write:

CelebrityPress™,
520 N. Orlando Ave, #44,
Winter Park, FL 32789

or call 1.877.261.4930

Visit us online at www.**CelebrityPressPublishing**.com

IGNITE
YOUR BUSINESS
TRANSFORM
YOUR WORLD

TABLE OF CONTENTS:

FOREWORD

Never doubt that a small group of thoughtful, committed citizens can change the world. Indeed, it is the only thing that ever has.
~ *Margaret Mead*

Each year, as a professional speaker, award-winning marketing coach and strategist and author, I have the distinct opportunity to reach thousands of entrepreneurs and small business owners to teach and inspire them to *'ignite their business and transform their world'*. When you change your circumstances, the circumstances of the world change. But first, as Gandhi said, "You must be the change you wish to see in the world." It all starts with you.

That is my mission. My big "WHY" as we call it. My purpose for living. To inspire you to step up as a leader in your business, in your community and set an example for what is possible in life.

The world is in a time of massive transformation and evolution. There is a shift in human consciousness occurring even as you read these words. There is quite a bit of evidence of massive breakthroughs occurring: the appearance of stunningly gifted children in unprecedented numbers, the emergence of innovative and integrated healing modalities, people becoming less "religious" and more "spiritual," and the dawning of new communities and social structures based on servant leadership and other partnership principles. And this is not just being talked about in the metaphysical world.

International leaders are seeking spiritual guidance from healers and intuitives in droves. Even our national treasure Oprah regularly speaks about the evolution of consciousness and hosted Eckhart Tolle and his book "A New Earth" on her first ever webinar series that was attended by millions of individuals ready for a spiritual awakening. As of 2009, over 5 million copies have been sold.

This trend cannot be ignored. As Tolle says, *"Humanity is now faced with a stark choice: Evolve or die. ... If the structures of the human mind remain unchanged, we will always end up re-creating the same world, the same evils, the same dysfunction."*

As leaders and entrepreneurs, there has been a universal call to arms for us to step up in consciousness. The universe is demanding it because as human consciousness exponentially increases, Earth will also undergo a significant–and observable–transformation.

In America with the financial crisis, entrepreneurs are going to save the economy. Entrepreneurs have the power to turn this around. We change the way that people think about what is possible. We have a clear vision of what is possible for all humans. Entrepreneurship is key to growth and job creation in America. Small companies earn 50% of the GDP and provide 50% of all jobs.

This book is a compilation of the leaders who have stepped

up in consciousness to ignite their business and change the world and who are challenging you to do the same.

It is time for you to stand in your light. What are you waiting for?

XOXO

Kelly K. O'Neil

www.kellyoneil.com

CHAPTER I

PROSPERITY WITH PURPOSE: HOW 'PLAYING BIG' SERVES THE WORLD

BY KELLY K. O'NEIL

After being in the personal development and business development industries as a speaker, author and coach for longer than the last decade, I see that there are two schools of thought.

There are the diehard capitalist entrepreneurs who tend to go to events that are all about making money, and then there are the spiritual events where everyone goes to meditate and love one another.

My work lies at the juxtaposition of those two worlds. I have helped build companies to multimillion dollar levels and I have done work for non-profits. At this point in my career, I am much more passionate about conscious entrepreneurship. A broad definition of a conscious entrepreneur is someone who merges their life purpose with their business to create a livelihood that is spiritually fulfilling and a direct path to freedom.

In 2009, I started a new company called Kelly O'Neil International, Inc. The tagline for that business is Ignite Your Business. Transform Your World™. That is where the title for this book came from.

Kelly O'Neil International is a coaching and training company that serves female entrepreneurs who are passionate about the work they are doing in the world. They know it is time to get their message out there so they can help you achieve your biggest goals and transform the lives of the millions of people in the process. But they aren't quite sure how. And frankly, it can be frightening for us to step out into the spotlight in such a big way. So instead, they have been 'playing it safe' and 'playing small' and hoping no one noticed. Not only are they hiding their gifts... their business is suffering. Does this sound familiar?

I started this company because I hold a very strong belief that it is equally important to help humanity and serve the world as I believe it is to serve you and your family. There is nothing glorious or enlightened about being poor, but helpful. In fact, I will take that a step further. **I believe it is your *responsibility* as an entrepreneur to build a thriving profitable business that serves the world in a way that enhances humanity and fosters abundance.**

Now…reread that last sentence. Notice where you feel that in your body. Is your tummy saying "HELL YES!" or does it make you want to lose your lunch? Do you feel angry? Do you feel afraid? Do you feel undeserving?

Now notice what you are saying to yourself. "No one will pay me big money." "Making money is not important." "Helping people isn't what my business is for. It is to make money."

Here is why that is a critical exercise. The way you feel about yourself and your business impacts the way you think. The way you think impacts your actions. Your actions impact your results – financially and in your ability to serve the world.

Are you getting the results that you desire? If not, it is time to step up your game.

Our world is at a crossroads. In their book, *Half the Sky: Turning Oppression into Opportunity for Women Worldwide* (Knopf), husband-and-wife Pulitzer Prize winners Nicholas Kristof and Sheryl WuDunn argue that the key to economic progress in the world lies in unleashing women's potential. Education is a key to change. When you educate one young girl or woman, she takes what she learns to her community—and when a community knows better, they do better.

As entrepreneurs, we can no longer be silent. We must stand up and share our voices, share our healing and support one another in this journey. YOU can no longer be silent.

YOUR TIME IS NOW...TO ALLOW COURAGE TO ECLIPSE FEAR

The first step to playing a bigger game is to make a decision to do it, and that takes immense courage. I know that may sound simple, but this is where 95% of entrepreneurs get stuck. So often, we take action without making a decision first. That renders any and all action useless.

Several years ago, I read a poem that changed my life. I now read it every single day and assign this same practice to my coaching students:

"Our deepest fear is not that we are inadequate.
Our deepest fear is that we are powerful beyond
measure. It is our light, not our darkness that most
frightens us. We ask ourselves, Who am I to be
brilliant, gorgeous, talented, fabulous? Actually,
who are you not to be? You are a child of God.
Your playing small does not serve the world.
There is nothing enlightened about shrinking
so that other people won't feel insecure around
you. We are all meant to shine, as children do.
We were born to make manifest the glory of God
that is within us. It's not just in some of us; it's in
everyone. And as we let our own light shine, we
unconsciously give other people permission to do
the same. As we are liberated from our own fear,
our presence automatically liberates others."
~ Marianne Williamson, A Return to Love

FEAR: False Evidence Appearing Real

I knew that playing small was not acceptable. It was not acceptable for my life, or the life of those individuals I am meant to serve. Was I afraid? Yes, but I had to reach deep and muster the courage. Being fearless isn't about being 100% unafraid. It is about being terrified, but jumping anyway. Every day, I jump anyway. When you share your gift in a profound way and shine your light, you provide your clients with permission to do the same. Each time we face our fear, we gain strength, courage, and confidence.

YOUR TIME IS NOW...TO EMBRACE THE LEADER WITHIN YOU

Every year, I speak all over the world on stages to entrepreneurs. I have spoken alongside brilliant entrepreneurs like Harvey McKay, Tony Hsieh, Jack Canfield, Mark Victor Hansen, Brian Tracy and Christopher Howard. More often than not, I am the only female taking the stage. I am part of an exclusive organization of the worlds leading speakers and authors. Until a few years ago, I didn't even receive an invitation to attend. When I finally did, out of a room of 125 of the nations elite, there were 10 women and 5 of them were assistants to the 'big' guys. That year, I began my mission and in 2010 we finally did a woman's panel at that event. It was touted as the best segment of the event. Where are all the women leaders?

More than ever before, the world needs women leaders - and we are transforming the way business is conducted. An analysis in Psychology Today of 45 leadership studies found that the best leaders are inspirational mentors who encourage their followers to develop their abilities and creatively change their own circumstances. Women, on average, are more likely than men to enact this "transformational" style. Previous research has shown the transformational style to be most effective, particularly when companies rely on innovation to stay competitive.

Transformational leadership is a leadership style that leads to positive changes in those who follow. Transformational leaders are generally energetic, enthusiastic and passionate. Not only are these leaders concerned and involved in the process; they are also focused on helping every member of the group succeed as well.

As an example, at my company we offer profit sharing programs. My company is about creating a WIN-WIN-WIN scenario – the customers win, the team wins and my company wins. It puts every team member in the place to choose their own income and fosters dedication to the vision.

IT ISN'T JUST MY OPINION, THE RESEARCH SHOWS IT ALL

If that doesn't convince you, consider this research. According to the Center for Women's Business Research, women currently control $14 trillion in assets—a number that is expected to grow to $22 trillion within the next 10 years. Women also make up 43 percent of the North American affluent segment, which isn't necessarily surprising when you consider that women are starting businesses at twice the rate of men (based on Merrill Lynch research). As of 2010, there are over 10.6 million women-owned businesses employing 19.1 million people and generating $2.5 trillion in sales. Women business owners employ 35% more people than all the Fortune 500 companies combined – how many of your client-businesses are women-owned?

According to new data projections from The Guardian Life Small Business Research Institute, future job growth will be created primarily by women-owned small businesses. Guardian's research shows that by 2018 women entrepreneurs will be responsible for creating between 5 million and 5.5 million new jobs nationwide. That's more than half of the 9.7 million new jobs the Bureau of Labor Statistics expects small businesses to create, and about one-third of the total new jobs the BLS projects will be created nationwide in that time frame.

Why are we so successful? It is the way we run businesses. Studies indicate that women entrepreneurs are **diligently engaged in strategic and tactical facets of their business, proactively customer-focused, likely to incorporate community and environment into our business plans**, are **receptive to input and guidance from internal and external advisers...** and are **committed to creating opportunities for others.**

WHEN YOU LEAD YOU SERVE

Leadership is all about service. When you lead you serve. Those that serve learn an important lesson about leadership. Leadership empowers, lifts and inspires. When you serve others you empower, lift and inspire and you feel the satisfaction of making a difference for no other reason than it was the right thing to do.

It is time for you to embrace your inner leader.

YOUR TIME IS NOW...TO DO WHATEVER IT TAKES TO CREATE A HIGHLY PROFITABLE, CONSCIOUS BUSINESS

Creating profit is not just about living a luxurious lifestyle. Although there is absolutely nothing wrong with that. When you create a profitable business, you not only become a leader in the statistics above where you are creating jobs but you also then have the financial means to give back. When you follow a conscious business model, you seek to benefit both the external livelihood as well as the internal lives of the shareholders and employees.

I teach clients every day how to build highly profitable, conscious business models. If you want that information, feel free to visit my website: www.kellyoneil.com. Building the business model is just one step. But for many of us, we can take all the right action in the world, and it is not enough.

If you will take the time to line up your Energy, meaning create a vibration match between your desire and your belief, the Universe will deliver to you amazing circumstances and events toward your physical conclusions. However, if you proceed with action before you have aligned your Energies of belief and desire, there is not enough action in the world to make any real difference."
~ Abraham

DEVELOP A LOVE AFFAIR WITH MONEY

Many of us, especially women, do not have a healthy relationship with money. We are taught by those in our lives that we don't deserve money or it is hard to make money. Or that by earning money you are taking it away from someone else and it isn't spiritual to earn money..blah, blah, blah. These are all false and limiting beliefs that will keep you and your business 'playing small'.

If your bank account is not full, you likely have resistance to receiving abundance.

When people ask us how long does it take for something to manifest, we say, It takes as long as it takes you to release the RESISTANCE. Could be 30 years, could be 40 years, could be 50 years, could be a week. Could be tomorrow afternoon.
Abraham-Hicks

Your ability to create and retain wealth is determined by your relationship with money. Like everything on this planet, money is simply a form of energy which is attracted to the energy that is like itself. Your relationship with anything determines how much of that thing you are attracting or repelling. Money does not exist by itself, but it is always attached with the energy of the person who relates with it.

It all comes down to values. Wealthy people know that money is very important, that is why they have it. Poor people think money is not important, that is why they lack it. Can you imagine if you kept telling your 'significant other' or your children that they are not important, how long do you think they are going to stay with you? What you appreciate, appreciates in value. What you do not appreciate, depreciates in value.

Here is where most people get trapped. Your motivation for making money is vital. If your motivation for making money comes from fear (lack), anger or the need to prove yourself, then money will never bring you happiness. Anger and the need to prove yourself are also forms of fear. It is a state of being where you feel you don't have something and therefore you need to fight to get it. It is to intend and act from a place of fear. The opposite is to intend and act from a place of love. It is a state of being where you are whole and doing what brings you joy. This is where you have the greatest power to be of service and attract the most money

There is nothing enlightening about denouncing wealth. The more money you have, the more you can circulate back into society and be a part of the abundance cycle.

Try this money exercise I assign to my clients developed by Louise Hay. Everyday for 10 minutes look yourself in your eyes in the mirror and say:

> *I am one with the Power that created me. I am totally open and receptive to the abundant flow of prosperity that the Universe offers. All my needs and desires are met before I even ask. I am Divinely guided and protected, and I make choices that are beneficial for me. I rejoice in other's successes, knowing there is plenty for us all.*
> *~ Louise Hay*

BE GRATEFUL

> *God gave you a gift of 86,400 seconds today. Have you used one to say "thank you?"*
> *~ William A. Ward*

One of the things that has had the biggest effect on my life is the realization of the power of gratitude. Truly being grateful for everything I have. It has affected everything. It has made me a more positive person. A more productive person. A better friend. A better coach. A happier person.

There's no doubt in my mind that the simple act of gratitude on a regular basis will change anyone's life, positively and immediately. If you look at what you have in life, you'll always have more. If you look at what you don't have in life, you'll never have enough.

This is a value I instill in those around me. In fact, when my friends and family sit down to eat at night, a ritual around our table is to tell everyone one thing that we are grateful for. I often have my team and my clients create a gratitude list of 25 things they are grateful for. At night when I lay my head on the pillow, I thank God for all of the gifts in my life including the ones that are posing themselves as challenges. In fact, especially the ones that are posing as challenges.

> *"Life will give you whatever experience is most helpful for the evolution of your consciousness. How do you know this is the experience you need? Because this is the experience you are having at the moment."*
> ~ *Eckhart Tolle*

Living in a state of gratitude is perhaps the most powerful key for a woman to stay in positive mindset. The reason for that, we now know, is that the part of the brain that is associated with feeling gratitude is not the same part of the brain that experiences fear, and that when one of those is sort of switched on, the other one automatically switches off. The way to be fearless is to start focusing on things for which you are grateful.

GIVE BACK

With this new shift in business, I believe that we are moving away from competition and moving toward collaboration. If you believe in abundance, I mean really believe in abundance, than you know there is more than enough to go around. What would the world be like if we all helped each other lift one another up, instead of tearing each other down?

I watched a movie several years ago called *Pay It Forward*. The movie is about a school social studies assignment that leads to social changes that spread from city-to-city. Assigned to come up with some idea that will improve mankind, a young boy decides that if he can do three good deeds for someone and they in turn can "pay it forward" and so forth, positive changes can occur.

In my company, we provide free content and tele-courses to entrepreneurial women who are just starting out. You can check that out on my website at www.kellyoneil.com. We also partner with KIVA.org to microfinance loans for budding entrepreneurs around the world. Not only does my company donate, but I also encourage our clients to donate as well. You can learn about Kiva at www.kiva.org.

What are ways you could 'pay it forward' and give back in your business?

YOUR TIME IS NOW...IT IS YOUR TIME TO SHINE

If you are reading this, it is no accident. Think of this chapter as a guardian angel tapping on your shoulder – reminding you of what you already know has been inside you waiting to come out. The world needs you and needs your gifts. It is time for you to step up and shine your light on the world.

ABOUT KELLY

Award winning author, speaker and coach Kelly O'Neil, is passionate about helping entrepreneurs think big, play bigger and step out into the spotlight to build highly profitable businesses that help create transformation in the world so they may live a truly extraordinary life. Kelly is the author of "Visionary Women Inspiring the World: 12 Paths to Personal Power" (Skyward, 2005). She has given thousands of media interviews to outlets that include *The Wall Street Journal, CNN, Bloomberg, Associated Press, The New York Times, USA Today, Time, Business Week, Forbes, Fortune, and even MTV*. She also appears regularly as a speaker at professional associations, as well as national and international conferences. Known for her devotion to excellence, Kelly's company has won several awards, including the PR Compass Award for Outstanding Public Relations and The ADDY Award for Branding. In addition, her company was named one of the 500 most innovative companies in America by Mega Marketing Guru Seth Godin. Kelly personally was honored by the presidential counsel with the National Leadership Award. You can learn more about Kelly O'Neil International at www.kellyoneil.com and download our free gift.

CHAPTER 2

BUILDING YOUR BRAND SOUND

– 3 WAYS AUDIO BRANDING IMPACTS YOUR CLIENTS, YOUR REPUTATION, AND YOUR BOTTOM LINE

BY FELICE KELLER

Almost a year ago, I was waiting for a teleseminar to begin that would feature one of the country's most respected life coaches and business strategists. My mind was wandering but immediately jolted back to the present when the background music started. It was not a motivating pop song or refined classical music. Instead it was ragtime with its "boom-chick" bass, which felt outdated, unsophisticated, and completely out-of-line with her trendsetting, upscale brand. I am confident she did not pick this music and probably just let the teleseminar organizers take care of song selection, but my perception of her was still affected. Had I not been recommended to her by a colleague, I might have hung up.

I began thinking...how many potential clients are subconsciously taking her less seriously and spending less money on her products and events? How much money was she leaving on the table? It was on that day I realized that there was a huge need for all businesses, not just huge corporations, to develop a clear and effective audio branding strategy.

In the following pages, you will learn about three ways in which utilizing music can truly improve your business by creating memories, improving the customer experience, and inspiring action to increase sales.

INSPIRED BY SONG

The impact of music and the emotions it evokes has always inspired me. While other kids were playing sports, I was taking piano lessons, singing in the Mercer Island Children's Choir, preparing for ballet, tap and jazz recitals, or re-writing the words to my favorite songs. I spent hours in a quest to make "perfect" mix tapes. Whether they were to send to friends from summer camp to remind them of our adventures together, or to create a soundtrack for a certain event like "Senior Road Trip," I would notice that experiences would come and go, but the music remained.

I went to college and earned my degree in creative writing, then, after working as a public relations specialist and newspaper reporter, went on to earn my MBA in marketing. I moved out to Los Angeles, taking a job as a fundraising director for a large local charity, and had the pleasure of working with one of our donors, Ray Evans, whom I learned had written classics like "Silver Bells" and "Que Sera Sera." He encouraged me to follow my songwriting dreams, and by the next year I was a professional songwriter, working in Nashville and Los Angeles. Through the years, I have been honored to collaborate with the best in the music industry, co-write with Grammy winners, and work as an on-air music reporter for XM Radio.

In 2008, I walked down the aisle to a song I wrote with the brilliant Andrea Stolpe, one of Faith Hill's writers, and was overwhelmed by its power to completely transform my wedding and the experiences of everyone there. Our guests were so moved that many expressed their dream of someday having a song of their own. After doing some research, I realized that unless people worked in the music business or were directly connected to someone who was, they didn't have access to making those dreams come true. I knew I had the network, the drive, and the passion to connect others with award-winning songwriters, top musicians and producers, and ultimately a song of their own. My company, Felice Keller Productions, was born.

Armed with my songwriting experience, business background and marketing skills, I committed to excellence and took every opportunity to learn. I began attending conferences targeting entrepreneurs, buying helpful information products, and listening in on teleseminars. Although we were primarily working with clients to create original, custom songs for their most special personal moments such as anniversaries, father/daughter wedding dances, and Bar/

Bat Mitzvahs, the teleseminar I referenced earlier opened my eyes and ears to the power of audio branding. I knew I could help business owners create and/or select music to serve as a brand asset instead of a liability. Felice Keller Productions expanded our services to become a leading force in audio branding.

WHAT IS AUDIO BRANDING?

In the audio branding 'bible,' "*Sonic Branding*," British author Daniel M. Jackson gives a fascinating history of music as it relates to branding as well as examples of audio branding at its best. Jackson, who defines audio branding (also known as sound branding, sonic branding, acoustic branding) as: "the creation and consistent management of distinct, memorable, flexible and honest brand identity and experience, in sound," notes that, "the vast majority of brands own no sonic branding and have given it very little thought." He explains that a distinctive edge is given to those who do, because they have the opportunity to create a "relationship with its audiences through their ears" (Jackson, 2004).

More than one thousand billion dollars is spent worldwide each year on how brands look, but less than 10 percent of the world's top brands have a "sensory branding platform," utilizing all five senses including sight, hearing, smell, touch, and taste (Treasure, 2007). Interestingly, that percentage is expected to increase to 35% in the next five years, and marketing experts are clear that no brand should be facing the 21st century without a clear statement of its sound.

Some of the most important elements of a brand's audio

blueprint include deliberate, targeted, and clear audio branding guidelines, an audio logo, product sound, hold music and the telephone experience, point of sale, mobile marketing, brand voice, brand music, and website audio. Nevertheless, a comprehensive strategy for a brand's audio expression would consider all touchpoints where customers, partners and even employees come into contact with the brand.

CREATING A MEMORY

In 1821, renowned English poet Percy Bysshe Shelley wrote, "Music, when soft voices die, vibrates in the memory." Amazingly, he realized that while hundreds of details fade from our minds through the years, music has the power to immediately transport us back to a moment of significance or convey an emotion. Consequently, progressive companies are now considering their audio choices to be a vital part of their brand strategy. The new thinking is that if a company cares what it's brand looks like, they should be just as concerned, if not more, with what it sounds like.

Consider this: most consumers may not be able to draw Nokia's logo or recall its tagline, but its ringtone (Nokia's audio logo) can be hummed by many of them. By actually making its audio logo the default ringtone and one of its product sounds, Nokia has become a leading force in the telecommunications industry.

While wildly underused, audio logos can be extraordinarily powerful. Another example is Intel, a company that sells microprocessors. In the 1980's, they were virtually unknown, with a product that was of little interest to the public. In fact, Intel needed to sell directly to other companies, such as IBM, who would use their technology in the building of computers, but they still invested in making the end customer care about and covet their products. It was the "Intel Inside" campaign and the corresponding five-note "signature ID audio-visual logo" that has taken Intel's products from commodity to necessity. Its consistent and strategic use for more than 15 years has given Intel one of the most recognizable audio logos in the world.

Other memorable audio logos include NBC's three chimes and MGM's lion's roar. My favorite? The single "ding" from Southwest Airlines. In my opinion, they have set a new standard for audio branding. That one tone, initially recognizable as a sound heard on flights before takeoff and landing on every airline, has become a symbol for Southwest. Most impressive is their ability to utilize it consistently, repeatedly, and in multiple customer touchpoints. On commercials, it's "ding, you are now free to move about the country." If you sign up for their free online or Smartphone notifications, you are alerted to fare sales with that same "ding." In fact, it's even called the DING! application. Last week, as I prepared to board a Southwest flight, I heard the agent scan my boarding pass. "Ding." Another reminder that I was flying Southwest. What was once simply a product sound of the airplanes is now an officially registered trademark of Southwest Airlines.

Jingles, though not as widely used in this advertising climate, are clearly memorable. From "I'd Love To Be An Oscar Mayer Wiener" to "You Deserve a Break Today at McDonalds," these brands are permanently etched in our minds. In fact, "I'd Like To Buy The World A Coke" was an original jingle for the Coca-Cola Company and became such a favorite that it was reworded and released by two bands, The New Seekers and The Hillside Singers, eventually breaking into the top 20 of the Billboard Top 100 (Billboard.com). And no matter what version of the song we hear, we most likely recall the television commercial and think peace, community and Coke.

As a side note, *The Wall Street Journal* reported in November 2009 that people can still remember and sing songs long after they have stopped recognizing names and faces, even after the brain ages and in extreme cases succumbs to Alzheimer's. It seems that there is no single center for music in the mind, but the prefrontal cortex (directly behind the forehead) appears to serve as a hub for music, memory and emotions. This is fortunate, as it is also one of the last regions of the brain to atrophy in Alzheimer's patients (Beck, 2009). Though once just theorized, the link between music and memory is now truly undeniable.

IMPACTING THE CUSTOMER EXPERIENCE

In addition to creating associations and memories, a company's implementation (or lack of implementation) of an audio branding strategy directly affects the customer experience. Studies show audio can change brand perception, brand loyalty, and overall comfort in an environment.

A study conducted in 2000 determined that music did indeed alter the atmosphere of a bank. It illustrated a positive correlation between the characteristics of music and the customer ratings of the company. In cases where the music was perceived as more optimistic, so was the bank. When no music was played, customers found the bank to be less dynamic and upbeat (North, Hargreaves, & McKendrick, 2000).

Also, many companies are noticing that the background music customers hear is impacting their wait time. This is seen both in brick-and-mortar locations as well as waiting on-hold on the telephone. An article in "The Psychology of Music" attributes this to the theory that music affects time perception. A university study showed that the use of music in waiting situations (versus waiting without exposure to music) leads to both "an underestimation of time spent" and an increase in time waiting before hanging up (Gueguen & Jacob, 2002).

Furthermore, a musically enhanced environment can also serve as a portal to relaxation and concentration. This may explain why so many business leaders, especially those in the transformational industry, utilize music during exercises and activities. They realize that clients are better able to get in the desired "zone" if specific music is played while journaling, brainstorming, meditating, writing, or completing worksheets.

The results are so tangible in improving the ability to learn, create, and explore that our clients are hiring us to create complete playlists for their workshops, seminars, and other important events. In fact, for similar reasons of evoking emotion and creating the most ideal environment, brides are asking us to help select the songs played throughout their wedding ceremony to ensure the soundtrack of 'their day' lives on. Researchers are still looking at specific components of music and finding that those such as tempo, familiarity, volume level, and genre to be the most influential.

A product's actual sound also has an amazing impact on the customer experience. It may be hard to believe but specific teams are assembled to create all kinds of product sounds from the door-slam of a Mercedes-Benz to the unmistakably loud thump-thump-thump of the Harley-Davidson motorcycle. From the "sss" of espresso brewing at your local cafe to the ringtone on your mobile phone.

In fact, Stewart Copeland, composer and former drummer for The Police, was commissioned to come up with a unique "theme" for the BlackBerry Bold. "The result was a signature five-note melody which Copeland expanded into a percussive minute-long track simply named 'Bold'... A softer version with a fade-in is used as an 'alarm tone' to gently rouse the Bold owner from his or her slumber, while six variations – which are actually excerpts from various parts of the Bold theme – are available as ring tones" (Flynn, 2008).

Companies like Research In Motion, creator of the Black-Berry, are realizing the impact of an effective audio branding strategy and paying big money to capitalize on that. Also, there is a coolness factor when associating with a rock star that may shift the customers' perception of the brand.

A company's audio expression gives us, usually subconsciously, clues as to their brand promise and anticipated experience. To be effective, audio must be congruent with all other branding activities. Imagine walking into a spa called "Relax," only to hear AC/DC playing or watching an exclusive fashion show in New York that featured Barry Manilow. Something would seem "off," and you would be puzzled and conflicted, wondering what the brand actually represents. This is why it is essential that the client audio experience be protected.

INSPIRING ACTION AND SALES

Most exciting to business owners and marketing professionals are studies that have indicated that background music can play a major role in customer behaviors leading to purchase decisions.

In 1998, a British wine shop did an experiment, and for a number of days played French and German music, alternating between the two. The results were significant. On French-music days, the French wine outsold the German wine by a ratio of four to one. On German-music days, German wine outsold the French by a ratio of three to one (Franus, 2007). While further and more extensive research must be done, the implications of this are fascinating. It is not unreasonable that online shopping sites could soon be playing specific music while customers are considering certain purchases.

According to Julian Treasure, Chairman of The Sound Agency, "the top-line summary is that music does significantly affect people; it can speed them up or slow them down, and it can change their mood. As a result they behave differently - and, most importantly for the retailers in question, it affects the amount of time and money they spend in the establishment" (Treasure, 2007).

Studies focused on tempo have indicated that shoppers spent more time and money in a slow tempo retail environment (Milliman, 1982). When in a restaurant environment, customers in the slow music condition took more time to eat their meals and spent more money on beverages compared to those listening to fast-paced music (Milliman, 1986).

Another study conducted in a wine shop examined the impact of Top-Forty versus classical music being played on Friday and Saturday evenings for a three-month period. Though the amount of "shelf items examined, and purchased" and shopping time did not vary by music genre, research concluded that patrons spent more money when the classical music was playing in the background (Areni & Kim, 1993). Interestingly, customers were not buying a greater quantity of wine, but selecting more expensive bottles. It was unclear to researchers whether classical music promoted the purchase of expensive wine or Top-Forty reduced more pricey selections. Nevertheless, the difference was significant.

You may think your customers' buying decisions (and your own) are not impacted by music, but you would probably be wrong. In the first wine store experiment where French music led to 80 percent of shoppers selecting French wine, only 1 out of 44 customers acknowledged the music as a reason for buying the wine. Why is this important to note? Because you can't just ask your customers to self-report on the motivation behind their buying habits. While they cannot be confident that music may be affecting their buying decisions, you can.

NEXT STEPS: DEVELOPING YOUR OWN AUDIO BRAND

It is clear, even from this brief discussion, that audio has become an essential component in marketing and branding successful companies and products.

So how do you, as a business leader, start developing your own brand sound? At Felice Keller Productions, we walk our private clients though a distinctive three-phase process.

1. Creating Your Audio Branding Strategy

The first and arguably the most important step, developing your audio branding strategy, is often the most overlooked. Just as you need to know what city you want to visit in order to consider your travel options and make the best arrangements, the same can be said about developing your strategy: it will serve as a guide when choosing why, where, and how to express your sound.

Begin by evaluating whether you are creating a signature sound for a product, personal brand, or entire company. For example, a company like Nestlé has audio branding strategies for separate products and brands. Nestlé's Kit Kat's "Gimme a Break" jingle conveys very different messages from their Carnation's "Carnation Instant Breakfast... you're gonna love it in an instant." Or if trying to build an audio strategy for the George Foreman Grill, issues of Foreman's own personality and perceived attributes would have to be taken into account.

As in all branding efforts, the starting point in developing audio identity is clarifying your product offering, your target market, and the emotions and ideas you are trying to convey. The mission is to generate a consistent message across touchpoints, from your website and hold music to advertising and live events. Look at your logo, your customers and clients, your competitors, your brand values, and your brand promise. What are you trying to communicate to your customers, employees, and partners?

If you have a solid branding and marketing plan, you are at a significant advantage. Regardless, though, you need to evaluate your current audio choices. What does your company or product sound like? Is the audio you are currently using representative of the message you are trying to convey? Is it properly licensed?

You may think you are starting with a clean slate, but you would be surprised how many audio decisions have already been made, even if not by you. What does your hold music sound like? Is your receptionist (or auto-receptionist) a male or female? Do they have an accent? Are they speaking in a formal manner or more casually? Whether you knew it or not, your company's phone system is conveying messages about your value, your products, and your employees.

On one occasion, a colleague's auto-receptionist changed from a sophisticated British woman's voice to that of a younger American girl overnight. I assumed she had decided to target a new audience or re-evaluate her brand. On the contrary. It turned out her new assistant was reworking the phone system and decided the default voice sounded fine. This business owner, like so many of us, doesn't listen to her own hold music or have exposure to the receptionist or auto-receptionist. How often do you call yourself? With dozens of clients calling each day, her company was sending an unintended message of change.

After great research, goal development, and evaluation of your current audio branding, it is time to establish your audio brand guidelines in what I refer to as your "Brand Sound Blueprint." This is where you create a clear, well-thought out, 'big picture' strategy incorporating your findings and crafting your vision. A successful brand strategy requires consistency, clarity, distinctiveness, significance, flexibility, scalability, suitability, and the communication of your brand values.

While it is essential to create this written plan, it is often helpful to express your brand in a more tangible way. In our process, that happens in the development of a BrandBox. Whether it is a shadow box, a decorative filing box, or even a shoebox, the idea is to fill it with things that reflect your brand. Fabrics. Colors. Other products and items. Words cut out from magazines. Pictures. Anything that connects you with your brand.

Now comes the fun part. Honing in on your actual sound. Make a mix CD of music that you feel represents your brand. Madonna, Aerosmith, Johann Sebastian Bach, Sheryl Crow, selections from movie soundtracks… anything. Though you likely won't use these exact tracks to promote your company, they will serve as a guide when selecting the music you will utilize. Also consider identifying sound effects that are appropriate. For example, if you are promoting suntan lotion, you could choose the crashing of the waves, the sound of the product being sprayed, squirted, or applied, or a relaxing "ahhh" of someone knowing they are protected from the sun's rays while basking in its glow.

Then consider who may have your ideal brand voice: a voice that would be answering your calls, introducing you on stage, featured in your advertisements? Is it a male or female? Does he sound more like Sean Connery, James Earl Jones, Bill Clinton, Zac Efron or George Clooney? Or does she sound more like Barbara Walters, Dolly Parton, Oprah Winfrey, Sarah Jessica Parker, or Miley Cyrus? Make a separate CD featuring your favorite brand voices or bookmark pages online where you can hear and easily reference voices. Between podcasts, media streaming, and interviews on celebrity websites, you have endless access.

By filling your BrandBox and clearly outlining your audio branding strategy, you have thought through some of the most important questions, made essential decisions, and created an invaluable resource.

2. Finding the Best Music: Song Selection or Creation

Once your strategy is in place, it is time to decide whether you will ultimately be using existing audio or creating your own. Although you may want to use your favorite Beatles song in your promotional activities, you are probably out of luck unless you have millions of dollars to spend. This is because of copyright law and the requirement you get the permission of the song's owners, who are not necessarily its songwriters. All parties must find mutually agreeable terms and negotiate an acceptable fee.

The good news is that there are existing songs that are not as expensive to license. You may be able to work out a deal with your favorite independent artist. Also, you can do an online search for "small business music license" and find resources where you can listen to music snippets and decide if they would be a good fit for your brand. This will potentially be a time-consuming endeavor as it can be a challenge to find songs that relay your brand's message and values perfectly.

Another option is to hire a company like ours that walks you through the audio branding process and finds songwriters, producers and musicians to flawlessly execute your strategy by creating custom audio for you. While we are fortunate to have a team of hit songwriters, award-winning composers, marketing leaders, and advertising professionals, many companies are not. Though they may be able to create music you personally enjoy, it is vital they understand your market and express your brand appropriately. A company like ours works with businesses of all sizes to create their perfect brand sound with the *specific intention* of helping them build their brand identity, connect with their ideal clients, and increase revenue.

One benefit of using original music is that it has no other associations to brands, artists, etc., but more importantly, if commissioned by your company, it will remain your audio property. Part of the challenge, for example, of Levi's using Willie Nelson's "You Are Always On My Mind" in their commercials, is that it is almost impossible to make it consistent and sustainable. The licensing fees will continue to rise, and just when a brand identity is created, it can be broken. In some cases, even transferred to another company.

Another advantage of commissioning music is making it flexible, scalable, and relevant. For example, if you expanded into a new market, you could potentially use the same song and have it re-arranged and re-recorded to sound more hip-hop, R&B, country, or even classical. Several large corporations have done this, even creating a Christmas-sounding arrangement for the holiday season.

Whether you choose existing or original music, remember the audio you select to represent your company, like your logo, should be distinctively recognizable and consistently used.

3. Expressing Your Brand

In this final step, it's time to execute. We identify the touchpoints where customers, partners, and even employees are exposed to your brand. Consider everything from your website, your point-of-sale location, trade shows, speaking engagements, presentations, teleseminars, waiting on-hold, and the sound your product makes when in use.

Then commission or select and license the necessary brand elements such as an audio logo, a brand song or anthem, and instrumental introduction.

Remember, the objective is to utilize audio to serve as a memory trigger that connects your brand or product with a positive feeling while creating confidence and familiarity.

CONCLUSION

As I conveyed earlier, if you care about how your business looks, it is imperative you care about the way it sounds. People can choose to close their eyes but it is impossible to close their ears, making the audio you select absolutely invaluable.

It is clear that utilizing a strategic audio brand strategy can truly improve your business by creating memories, impacting the customer experience, and inspiring action to increase sales.

I wish you great success in your audio branding. Please feel free to contact me if our company can be of service to yours or simply to update me on your progress.

Now get to work and remember: make your sound memorable, consistent, and above all, a perfect reflection of your precious brand.

Felice Keller Productions
: www.felicekeller.com
: fk@felicekeller.com
(818) 424-SONG (7664)
3940 Laurel Canyon Blvd. #1143
Studio City, CA 91604

. . . .

Works Referenced

- Areni, C. S., & Kim, D. (1993). The Influence of Background Music on Shopping Behavior: Classical Versus Top-Forty Music in a Wine Store. *Advances in Consumer Research , 20.*

- Beck, M. (2009, November 16). A Key for Unlocking Memories. *Wall Street Journal.*

- Billboard.com. (n.d.). *Chart History.* Retrieved May 10, 2010 from Billboard: http://www.billboard.com/#/artist/hillside-singers/chart-history/21858

- Flynn, D. (2008, August 4). Must Hear: Stewart Copeland Puts Message In a Bottle for BlackBerry Bold Owners. *APC .*

- Franus, N. (2007, April 26). *Building Sound Value Through the Strategic Use of Sound.* Retrieved May 10, 2010 from AIGA: http://www.aiga.org/content.cfm/building-brand-value-through-sound

- Gueguen, N., & Jacob, C. (2002). The Influence of music on Temporal Perceptions in an On-Hold Waiting Situation. *Psychology of Music , 30,* 210-214.

- Jackson, D. (2004). *Sonic Branding: An Introduction.* Palgrave Macmillan.

- Milliman, R. E. (1986). The Influcence of Background Music on the Behavior of Restaurant Patrons. *Journal of Consumer Research,* 286-289.

- Milliman, R. E. (1982). Using Background Music to Affect

the Behavior of Supermarket Shoppers. *Journal of Marketing* , *46* (2), 86-91.

- North, A., Hargreaves, D., & McKendrick, J. (2000). The Effects of Music on Atmosphere in a Bank and a Bar. *Journal of Applied Social Psychology* , 1504-1522.
- Treasure, J. (2007). *Sound Business.* Management Books 2000 Ltd.

ABOUT FELICE

An award-winning songwriter based in Los Angeles, Felice Keller is the CEO of Felice Keller Productions, a trendsetting company that specializes in creating perfect moments through music. For companies, she develops and implements cutting-edge audio branding strategies. For individuals, she makes special occasions extraordinary by commissioning hit writers for artists like Taylor Swift, Barbra Streisand, and even Frank Sinatra to create and record original, custom songs.

Felice works with many of the most successful players in the music industry. Several of her songs are currently being recorded and others are being showcased in a variety of television and film projects. Her music was prominently featured on MTV's "The Hills" and "Laguna Beach."

She is known for her talent in connecting the right people with each other and furthering the careers of songwriters and artists. She has executive produced albums, placed music on hit television shows and Billboard-charting albums, and continues to be a valuable resource to many.

Raised on Mercer Island, Washington (near Seattle), she graduated Phi Beta Kappa from the University of Arizona and went on to earn her MBA in marketing at the University of Washington. She has worked in radio and concert promotions, public relations, and as a freelance writer, interviewing notable individuals such as Steven Spielberg, Jim Brickman (Grammy-nominated pianist), and Jeffrey Seller (producer of the Tony award-winning "Rent").

In addition to running Felice Keller Productions, Felice is an on-air reporter for Musicians' Radio on XM. She is a philanthropist and active volunteer for organizations including the Venice Family Clinic, Juvenile Diabetes Research Foundation, and Step Up Women's Network, where she is an Executive Board Member.

CHAPTER 3

TEN WAYS TO IGNITE AND TRANSFORM YOU

BY J.W. DICKS, ESQ.

Most of us don't have time to transform the world... or so we think.

In fact, most people believe there is actually very little we can personally do about the problems in the world, whatever view we hold them to be. The results of that belief is often that no action is taken one way or the other to bring about transformations and nothing is changed.

The truth is that the world is frequently transformed by individuals, and some recent examples in business are Google founders Larry Page and Sergey Brin and Facebook founder Mark Zuckerberg and his college classmates. Depending on your view of their companies you may not like the transformations, but clearly what they have accomplished has transformed the lives of people throughout the world.

Even still, the resistance to act by us "average Joe's and Jane's" is often still the same. We get caught up in our own time and space working to ignite our own life and business, forgetting that thoughtfully, our actions could change the world, or at least parts of it.

I am reminded of the Wally Amos (Famous Amos Cookies) story of the young boy walking down the beach, picking up starfish that washed ashore and throwing them one by one back into the water before they died.

"You're wasting your time," said an observer as he passed by, amused by the boys actions. "You can't save them all, you know."

"Saved that one," the boy replied, picking up another starfish and casting it back into the ocean.

The observer was right of course, but the boy was smarter. We can't save all of the starfish nor the pelicans coated by the oil spill. And we can't transform the entire world from all of its problems at the same time. It isn't possible. What we can do is ignite what is under our control… our business. And in igniting our business, use methods that not only boost business, but at the same time transform others both directly and indirectly. Let me give you some ideas exactly how you can start today to both ignite your business and transform the world.

It all starts with getting out and 'stirring the pot' a little bit.

In fact, if the truth be known, marketing and igniting your business doesn't take much more than persistent effort.

1. **Write a book.** I have written over 15 books and had the good fortune to see a number of them become a best seller. There is, in many ways, nothing more powerful to ignite a business or transform the world than the power of a book. Each book I have written had a positive effect on my business - if for no other reason than it brought motivation and excitement to what we were doing at the time. Can I say that any of these books have transformed the world? No! Does that matter? Again, no it does not. In my case, I am simply a "starfish thrower". What I hope is that my action of sharing "thoughts on things learned", will help someone else to take another action and who knows what happens. For example, perhaps this chapter will motivate you to write your own book, and that in turn motivates another.

The problem for most people when they think of writing a book is that it seems a daunting task. The secret to actually getting it written is to break the task down into smaller parts. A page a day for 6 months is a decent book. Write one page a day for an entire year and you have a big book. If that seems too much, then just commit to writing a chapter size special report on something you are knowledgeable in, and share it free with as many people as you can. Alternatively, put together your own group of writers and each do a chapter as we have done with this book. There are lots to learn and share in the process, and the more you write, the better you get at doing it.

A more sophisticated version of producing content of

your own and sharing with others we call content marketing. Entire businesses are built around it. If you have something to say and we all do, say it and get it out to the world. Some who read your content will want to do business with you and some wont, but understand that you are affecting even the lives of those that don't do business with you, because they may take your idea and do something else with it that changes their life or the lives of others. I have met many people over the years who told me they had read something that I wrote and the effect it had on them or their business. It is like you are throwing a rock in a pond and watching it spread through the ripples.

2. **Put on a seminar.** Yea, I know…afraid of public speaking. Then don't do a seminar but hire someone else to deliver your information in seminar form. Seminars are a powerful medium and they consistently deliver. While this form of marketing channel can be expensive to put on yourself, it certainly doesn't have to be. There are many organizations always looking for good speakers or a great message for their meeting attendees. If public speaking is new to you consider joining a group like Toastmasters that have clubs and offer help to new speakers in most cities.

Public speaking can also lead to paid speaking or opportunities to present your products or services to an audience you would not otherwise reach.

3. **Hold a teleseminar or webinar.** The online world offers us tremendous opportunities to the traditional seminar which requires your presence outside your own environment. We hold both teleseminars and webinars

almost every week for both clients and prospects. The teleseminar is the easiest to produce because it requires little technology or equipment and since no one can see you, dressing up is optional. Webinars are different in that they usually are a combination of voice and slides, or video ...which requires a bit more production. Webinars produce a little stronger sales, but we use teleseminars more often, because they require so much less time to produce and get out to clients and prospects. In both cases you can record your productions for later playback or to deliver in other formats like CD and MP3, or transcribing them to provide a written version for those people who like their content delivered that way.

4. **Write a Newsletter.** If a book is one of my favorite forms of marketing, a newsletter is my favorite form of *continuity* marketing that keeps in touch with your clients over time. It gives you a consistent opportunity to ignite your audience with your vision and its reach can be worldwide - with relatively limited cost.

Newsletter production can be set to your schedule. The frequency can be daily, weekly, monthly, quarterly, or whenever you feel like it. I recommend that you pick a consistent frequency and stick with it. Most people who write newsletters for their business use a monthly schedule. Once again, the problem of producing a newsletter seems a big task but if you are writing about something you like, you will find that you get into a rhythm. Also, writing over the course of a month vs. last minute writing makes it easier and more fun.

The power of a newsletter is that it allows you to stay in touch with your clients on a regular basis and keeps your marketing fresh. Not everyone is ready to buy your product or service at any time, and a newsletter brings your message to them consistently; so it is present as your silent sales force when your prospect is ready to receive what you are offering.

Your newsletter is also an excellent pulpit for you to release your ideas to transform the world - be the topic 'green energy' or 'health care'. You have a group of readers, a platform and the opportunity so share. While some people think this makes you vulnerable to people who don't like your view point, the reality is that honestly sharing your thoughts without bashing others solidifies you with your readers who get to know you better as a person and not just a faceless business. This 'anchor of trust' more than makes up for any minor conflicts you might create with some readers.

5. **Join the world.** By joining the world, I mean be part of events on topics in which you are interested, whether large or small. By active participation, you are giving yourself an opportunity to have a good time, meet others who may be interested in what you do or say and have an opportunity to share. Our family, who works together, uses travel as an excellent opportunity to meet potential clients and at the same time expose ourselves to the needs of others in foreign countries. Mixing doing what you like with your business and doing good at the same time, is a terrific combination of marketing that is fun, rewarding and profitable.

6. **Blogging** is another form of writing, sharing and marketing that many critics think is a waste of time. Yet there are bloggers who have built million dollar busi-

nesses off the success of their blogs from endorsements, advertisings or the sale of products. My daughter has a web site she blogs on and shares ideas with mothers across the internet. As I was writing this article, she stopped me to say that she had just won a $1,000 contest just by getting her readers to vote on a picture she had submitted. She can't retire off the income but an extra grand for just asking your readers to vote for you proves the value of blogging and the fun of it.

7. **Email.** How many emails do you get a day? Too many, right? It's true, we all do but they are also opportunities to be responsive to the needs of your customers. I don't know how many emails I get but my partner counted his up and it typically hits in the 400 range that he has to answer. On each answer he has as his signature all of his contact information and sometimes a special marketing tag line. He isn't the only smart guy to take some advantage of emails for promotion either, because many others do it and you can too. Just go into your email control file and add a signature line to every email you send out. The more people that contact you from something you put in the line, the more you are going to enjoy sending and responding to emails. Now, even the dumb ones you get have potential.

8. **Podcasting.** Have you ever wanted to have your own radio show to share your thoughts with the world? Podcasting is the easiest way to do it because it is your show, you produce it and you can post it on your website, syndicate it or even video yourself talking on your show and send out the video of you "live" and entertaining. If you want to see some examples, check out podcast.com which list over 27,000 examples or pod-

castalley.com that has over 18,000.

9. **Video casting** is the podcast's big brother because all video is hot online and you can change your business fortunes fast. If you are good and get a hit like Gary Vaynerchuk – who used his goofy live video cast, called Wine Library TV, to promote his own family wine store and boost sales into the millions. YouTube.com and Google Video are two of the big sites on which you can post your own show - while you are building your audience and telling your story.

10. **Your own nonprofit organization.** This year my partners and I entered the nonprofit world, raised money and produced a video called *Jacob's Turn*. The seven-minute film is the story of a young boy with Down's syndrome who finally reaches the age to play organized baseball like his older siblings did. While a short film, it is a story of awakening, sharing, victory and blessings with gifts despite special needs. Our foundation is called Marketers for Good, and we have already received commitments from some of the biggest names in marketing to promote the film and its message to over a million people and direct TV to broadcast to over 60,000,000 homes. The message has ignited us and while it may not transform the world, it will transform its little piece. If you would like to view the film, you can do so at: JacobsTurn.com

ABOUT J.W.

J.W. Dicks, Esq. is America's foremost authority on using personal branding for business development. He has created some of the most successful brand and marketing campaigns for business and professional clients to make them the Credible Celebrity Expert in their field and build multi-million dollar businesses using their recognized status.

J.W. Dicks has started, bought, built, and sold a large number of businesses over his 39 year career and developed a loyal international following as a business attorney, author, speaker, consultant, and business expert's coach. He not only practices what he preaches by using his strategies to build his own businesses he also applies those same concepts to help clients grow their business or professional practice the ways he does.

J.W. has been extensively quoted in such national media as USA Today, The Wall Street Journal, Newsweek, Inc. Magazine, Forbes.com, CNBC.Com, and Fortune Small business. His television appearances include ABC, NBC, CBS and FOX affiliate stations around the country. He is the resident branding expert for Fast Company's internationally syndicated blog and is the publisher of Celebrity Expert Insider, a monthly newsletter targeting business and brand building strategies.

J.W. has written over 15 books, including numerous best sellers, and has been inducted into the National Academy of Best Selling Authors.

J.W. is married to Linda, his wife of 38 years and they have two daughters, a granddaughter and two Yorkies. J.W. is a 6th generation Floridian and splits time between his home in Orlando and beach house on the Florida west coast.

CHAPTER 4

CULTURAL TRANSFORMATION FROM THE GROUND UP:

BEING PART OF SOMETHING LARGER THAN YOURSELF

BY KENNETH COHN, MD, MBA, FACS
& THOMAS R. ALLYN, M.D., FACP

"Strategy may be nice, but culture eats strategy for lunch"
~ West-coast cardiac surgeon

INTRODUCTION

Culture encompasses the beliefs, habits, attitudes, stories, and assumptions that an organization develops to cope with issues. It reflects a shared view of the world and of effective methods for problem solving.

Entrepreneurs make time to reflect upon and shape organizational culture because a strong culture allows leaders to delegate tasks, knowing that outcomes will remain beneficial. Culture is dynamic, evolving with new experiences. It builds in stepwise fashion, one experience at a time (Cohn 2006).

The paradox of culture is that people who are part of entrepreneurial organizations enjoy bottom-up processes more than top-down edicts. They prefer being inspired to being supervised. The purpose of this chapter is to reflect on our experience of building a culture of collaboration from the ground up that has improved performance.

Collaboration has two meanings: derived from the Latin "collaborare" to work together, it also can imply betrayal, as in, "He is collaborating with the enemy." Therefore, although collaboration may have a negative connotation, it can also (Ardagh 2005):

- strengthen social networks
- nurture creative problem solving
- build trust
- provide and sustain hope

The following case illustrates the iterative journey of building a culture of collaboration from the ground up.

CASE PRESENTATION

Context

A West-coast community teaching hospital faced tumultuous times at the turn of the twenty-first century. New seismic regulations forced hospital leaders to build a new hospital costing hundreds of millions of dollars, but the services that would comprise the new hospital remained undefined. Surgeons who formed a competing local ambulatory surgical center took $5,000,000 from the hospital's revenue stream in their first year. Anesthesiologists who formed an outpatient, physician-owned pain center and gastroenterologists who formed their own endoscopy center took smaller but still worrisome bites out of the profitable services that supported the hospital's community mission.

At the same time, surgeons and anesthesiologists who previously viewed 'call' as part of their duty of care, began demanding additional compensation for coming to the hospital nights, weekends, and holidays. Tensions grew to the point that, at one meeting, a general surgeon told a urologist who was also a member of the hospital Board, "You're nothing but a hospital whore!"

Hospital sociology was also undergoing a tectonic shift: internists and family practice physicians, who used to make rounds at the hospital, were now entrusting inpatient care to hospitalists, a new type of physician who specialized in providing inpatient care (Cohn, Friedman, and Allyn 2007). This base of primary care physicians, who referred patients to hospital-based specialists, supporting both the specialists and the hospital, saw patients only in their offices, no longer came to the hospital, and, without action to keep them in the fold, could refer patients to any nearby hospital.

The business model was unsustainable, and conventional solutions no longer worked. The hospital and physicians needed to shift from an us-versus-them posture to a more collaborative approach.

Admitting Uncertainty

The Director of Medical Affairs (DMA) traveled to a presentation in which one of the authors (KHC) spoke on using a Medical Advisory Panel (MAP) for physicians to articulate a common vision for setting clinical care priorities for the community that they and the hospital served. The DMA thought that the benefits of coming to consensus outweighed the risks of continuing disharmony of the medical staff and financial erosion. He persuaded his fellow administrators to invite Cambridge Management Group (CMG), where Dr. Cohn worked at the time, to present at a medical staff retreat November 2002, where physicians, hospital leaders, and Board members could discuss issues and alternatives. They decided to begin the MAP process January 2003.

The major difference between the MAP process and traditional hospital-centric consulting processes is that physicians led the Medical Advisory Panel (MAP), facilitated by Dr. Cohn. The hospital CEO appointed the two MAP co-chairs, who picked 13 additional panelists. Like the co-chairs, the physician panelists were clinically savvy, had earned the respect of their colleagues, had good communication skills (or were teachable), and represented a variety of different disciplines and work settings, as discussed in the following section and depicted schematically in Figure 1.

A MAP member's journey: In his own words

I (TRA) am not a 'bureaucracy person'. I thought that the hospital was unable to change because it was too slow, cumbersome, reticent, and consensus-driven. I was skeptical because I felt that the hospital had never gotten the service concept down, and was incapable of fixing problems in a timely manner. Not wanting to commit to attending weekly 7 A.M. MAP meetings for the next six months, I said that I would attend the first meeting and make a decision afterward.

I quipped that *for this process to work, the hospital would have to undergo a cultural enema*, in that decision-making processes and operations would have to become significantly more transparent, efficient, and timely for physicians to feel that their ideas had merit. I returned to subsequent meetings only because I was impressed by the quality of my fellow panel members and was willing to trust the commitment made by the Board and CEO to give serious consideration to implementing the MAP recommendations.

I enjoyed the data-driven presentations, in which physicians from all major clinical areas discussed strengths, weaknesses, opportunities, and threats that they faced and recommended ways to improve care and to enhance physician-physician and physician-hospital communication. In addition, physicians on the MAP heard from the hospital CEO, Directors of Nursing and Finance, and the Chief Information Officer. We obtained a perspective of the hospital and the complexity of its operations that we never had appreciated before (Cohn 2006).

We evolved from a self-interested view of what the hospital should do for us as physicians *to a more empowered view of how the hospital could employ limited resources to improve care for our patients*. Through the process of discovery, we began to think and act more as long-term partners and co-owners than short-term customers and renters. The Medical Advisory Panel process allowed us to evolve beyond maintaining a level playing field for all physicians to leveraging hospital resources to meet community needs.

That clinicians who prided themselves on patient care could come to consensus on long-term priorities gave the Board and hospital administration the confidence to accept the MAP recommendations.

The results

Presentations from sections and departments to the MAP showed areas where the hospital could make an immediate improvement in the practice environment (i.e. Quick Fixes). For example, making sure that the on-call rooms where physicians stayed nights and weekends had clean linen and that physicians on call had parking places close to the hospital may not seem like a big deal, but taking care of such issues became a quick win that increased transparency and trust and made physicians feel that the time that they spent discussing and preparing their reports was not wasted.

The MAP panelists' report to the Board recommended the creation of an acute stroke center, an interdisciplinary palliative care program, and improvement of throughput in the Operating Room and Emergency Department, all of which were implemented within two years. Their report represented the first time that the hospital's top physicians had come to consensus on clinical priorities. Subsequent accomplishments were equally significant:

- A MAP panelist encouraged his orthopedic colleagues to consolidate vendors, which resulted in *$4.2 million hospital savings over three years*
- MAP spearheaded an ambitious program to limit sepsis mortality (i.e. death from overwhelming bacterial infection) by accelerating identification and treatment of septic patients with the rapid institution of antibiotics, which *halved mortality*

from overwhelming bacterial infection without changing any drugs and *saves over 40 lives per year*

- The acute stroke care center cares for over 300 patients per year – with outcomes that consistently exceed those of other acute stroke centers to which they compare their clinical outcomes
- As a result of progress made in improving the flow of surgical patients, the operating room staff received the 2009 GE Healthcare Centricity Perioperative Customer Innovation Award
- The MAP has continued to serve as an advisory "kitchen cabinet", meeting monthly with members of the hospital administration and reporting to the Board of Directors annually
- Several medical staff leaders (i.e. President, Vice-President, and Secretary of the Medical Executive Committee, the physicians' elected representatives) have emerged from their work as MAP panelists and presenters with a clearer idea of clinical priorities and healthcare complexity

CASE ANALYSIS

In his own words

The reason for my (TRA) change in behavior stems from the feeling that I am making my time count and that we are truly making a difference. Previous service on hospital committees felt like wasted time because I did not feel that anyone with the power to do anything was listening, and nothing was implemented in a timely fashion. No one person seemed accountable, and the communication loop rarely was closed.

We have built on previous successes and avoided death of innovation via the "slow no," or "let's study this some more...." The perception of hidden agendas on both sides has disappeared.

The MAP process has reinvigorated physician communication and patient care and has made me realize the value of pooling ideas and talent. Previously, *I did not realize how often we were talking 'at' each other, rather than 'to' each other.* Through the processes of dialogue, active listening, and discovery, which I called a combination of marriage counseling and group therapy, we are dealing with the complexities in healthcare administration and have begun to think, work, and act more interdependently than independently.

Implications for non-healthcare organizations

For a company's market value to exceed its book value, people and processes must come together to perform services that clients find valuable, such as solving problems, providing outstanding service, and creating experiences that exceed expectations. The case presentation illustrates how building a culture of collaboration from the ground up can accomplish these objectives and transform an organization. When leaders entice and persuade people to act, rather than resorting to fear and coercion, command-and-control techniques give way to a shared mission, vision, and values.

Pitfalls to overcome include:

- anxiety that "we don't usually work this way" and that the group will make an incorrect decision or recommendation
- impatience to get on with the process and impose

solutions, which decreases member buy-in and sabotages implementation

- inability or unwillingness to implement consensus solutions in a timely fashion, which makes members feel that their time was poorly spent; when professionals feel that their time is disrespected, they feel personally disrespected
- control issues: for this process to work, executives have to relax control to allow the advisory panel to morph into a functioning group which addresses needs, problems, and solutions; leaders eventually recognize that by loosening control, they gain influence; allowing systems to self-organize fosters engagement (Halbesleben 2010).

To overcome these pitfalls, we recommend the following 10-step process to build transparency, trust, and collaboration:

Ten Steps Toward Building a Culture of Collaboration from the Ground Up

1. Engage your top performers, regardless of irascibility.
2. Have ground rules to which the group commits, such as building on others' ideas, refraining from personal criticism, sharing responsibility for deadlines, developing win-win solutions, and respecting confidentiality (Cohn 2003).
3. Focus both on workplace pains that lead to suboptimal outcomes and past successes where 'people transcended silos' to achieve outstanding results (Cohn 2005).
4. Quantify the costs of continuing the status quo in terms of productivity, revenues, expenses,

outcomes, and workplace morale.

5. Visualize tangible benefits of improved processes and close the gap between steps 4 and 5.
6. Write each step of a frustrating process on a large post-it note; put the notes on a wall; ask the group how should, does, and could the process work, removing non-value added steps.
7. Prioritize efforts by first improving processes that will result in quick wins.
8. Celebrate success and build on the goodwill that success generates.
9. Chunk complex tasks into a series of outcome measures that have deadlines of no more than 2-3 weeks.
10. Repeat the process monthly in the beginning and at least quarterly thereafter.

CONCLUSION

In a study of over 1500 physicians, Brian Wong (2009) analyzed the top three items that survey participants desired:

- Meaningful work that makes a difference in people's lives
- A sense of community
- Regular, reliable, positive feedback that affirms participants' value

Do people with whom you work have similar needs? If so, experience the transformative benefits of a culture of collaboration by inviting people with whom you work to take a pivotal role in shaping *your* organization's culture.

. . . .

Works Referenced

- Ardagh A, Wilber K. 2005. *The Translucent Revolution: How People Just Like You Are Waking Up and Changing the World.* Indianapolis, IN: New World Library.
- Cohn KH, Friedman L, Allyn TR. 2007. The tectonic plates are shifting: cultural change versus mural dyslexia. Frontiers of Health Service Management. 24(1): 11-26.
- Cohn KH. 2006. Collaborate for Success! Breakthrough Strategies for Engaging Physicians, Nurses, and Hospital Executives. Chicago: Health Administration Press, 1-20.
- Cohn KH. 2005. Better Communication for Better Care: Mastering Physician-Administration Collaboration. Chicago: Health Administration Press, 24-29.
- Cohn KH, Peetz ME. 2003. Surgeon frustration: Contemporary problems, practical solutions. Contemporary Surgery. 59(2):76-85.
- Halbesleben JRB. 2010. *Managing Stress and Preventing Burnout in the Healthcare Workplace.* Chicago: Health Administration Press, 99.
- Wong B. A Prescription for Physician Reengagement. Futurescan 2009. Chicago: Health Administration Press, 23-26.

Figure I: The Medical Advisory Panel Process

Reprinted with permission from the American College
of Physician Executives

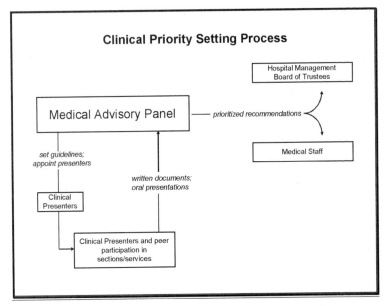

Cohn KH. The structured dialogue process: A successful approach for
partnering with physicians. Click, The Online Journal of the American
College of Physician Executives, 3/20/2002. www.acpe.org/Click.

ABOUT THOMAS

Dr. Thomas R. Allyn is a Board Certified Internist and Nephrologist who received his BA from Northwestern University, and MD from Columbia University's College of Physicians and Surgeons. He went on to do postgraduate training in Internal Medicine and Nephrology at the Massachusetts General Hospital and Harvard Medical School. Dr. Allyn then served as an Instructor in Medicine at Harvard Medical School and was the Director of the Acute Hemodialysis Service and the Acting Chief of Nephrology at Mt. Auburn Hospital, Cambridge, Massachusetts.

Since 1981, Dr. Allyn has been in the private practice of Internal Medicine and Nephrology in Santa Barbara, California where he is now the Chief of Nephrology and the Co-Director of the Acute Hemodialysis Service at Santa Barbara Cottage Hospital as well as the former Co-Chairman of their Medical Advisory Panel and a former member of the Long Range Strategic Planning Committee for the Cottage Health System. Dr. Allyn currently serves as Cottage Health System's Chairman of their Physician Hospital Alignment Work Group. Dr. Allyn is also the CEO and Medical Director of the Santa Barbara and Lompoc Artificial Kidney Centers and teaches Medical Students and Medical Residents at Santa Barbara Cottage Hospital as a Clinical Associate Professor of Medicine at USC as a member of their adjunct faculty.

ABOUT KENNETH

Dr. Kenneth H. Cohn is an internationally recognized thought leader in physician-hospital relations. The author of *Better Communication for Better Care* and *Collaborate for Success*, Dr. Cohn works with hospitals and health systems that want to work more interdependently with their physicians to boost revenues, cut expenses, and improve clinical outcomes.

He is a board-certified general surgeon who obtained his M.D. degree from Columbia University's College of Physicians and Surgeons and completed his residency at the Harvard-Deaconess Surgical Service. He was Assistant Professor of Surgery at SUNY Health Science Center at Brooklyn and later moved to Dartmouth-Hitchcock Medical Center as

Associate Professor of Surgery and Chief of Surgical Oncology at the VA Hospital at White River Junction.

With the change in the medical economic climate, Dr. Cohn entered the MBA program of the Tuck School at Dartmouth and graduated June 1998. He worked initially as a consultant at Health Advances, assisting 6 firms to commercialize new products. After joining the Cambridge Management Group in 1999, he led change-management and clinical priority setting initiatives for physicians at affiliated hospitals within the Yale New Haven, Banner Colorado, Cottage Santa Barbara, and Sutter Sacramento Health Systems.

In 2006, Dr. Cohn founded HealthcareCollaboration.com to help healthcare professionals improve care for their communities by working more interdependently.

Dr. Cohn remains clinically active, covering surgical practices in Maine, New Hampshire and Vermont. He has been mentoring physicians in leadership development since 1999, finding that physicians enjoy learning from fellow physicians.

Dr. Cohn's writing experience includes over 45 published articles in peer-reviewed healthcare journals. His article, "The Tectonic Plates Are Shifting: Cultural Change vs. Mural Dyslexia," won the Dean Conley Award in 2009 from the American College of Healthcare Executives for the best article in a healthcare management publication.

Dr. Cohn is the editor of *The Business of Healthcare,* a three-volume set, published in 2008 that comprises practice management, leading healthcare organizations, and improving systems of care. He is also the editor of *Improving Physician-Hospital Relations: A Field-Tested System,* a multimedia distance-learning program that helps hospital leaders engage physicians to improve care, improve operating room productivity, deal with disruptive physicians, and implement cutting-edge physician recruiting and retention strategies.

He blogs on topics related to healthcare collaboration at: http://healthcarecollaboration.com/blog and on strategies and tactics for disgruntled doctors at: http://thedoctorpreneur.com.

CHAPTER 5

THE PURPOSEFUL EXECUTIVE CAREER: LIVING YOUR LEGACY

BY MARIE GUTHRIE – EXECUTIVE CAREER STRATEGIST, CEO OF THE LEGACY TRACK

What did you want to be when you were growing up? When I was in elementary school in the mid 60's, I wanted to be a nun, a teacher and a nurse. I figured the perfect job for me was to be a nun who taught nursing and who entertained people on the weekends playing the guitar. After all The Singing Nun was at the top of charts appearing on the Ed Sullivan Show and The Flying Nun proved that anything was possible. My mother was a nurse and my oldest sister was a brand new elementary school teacher. I so wanted to be a patrol boy helping the younger kids cross the street, bossing them around, wearing that bright orange belt and holding that STOP Flag. It was the 60's. Patrol girls weren't allowed. I protested loudly, a very young early adopter of the women's liberation movement. Sister Mary Rogers was not amused. Not fair.

Viet Nam, Woodstock and Kent State changed everything. It was far more cool to play folk and war protest songs. All us good Catholic girls sang "I am Woman" at the top of our lungs as we protested the embarrassing long length of our uniforms and banished bloomers once and for all from PE. As the song says, "I can do anything" but what? The career interest test in '72 said I should be an engineer. Dad, the Nuclear Corrosion Engineer, questions the validity of the assessment. My High School Advisor said that means I should be a math major. Parents really like this idea. Phew, glad that is settled! Math it is.

So off to The Ohio State University I go with thousands of bright eyed freshmen eager to learn differential calculus in big auditoriums – BC – before calculators. I sail through theorems and integrals only to discover 25 credit hours later that I can't stand it and even worse the only career in Math is teaching, you guessed it, math. College Advisor says, no worries, get a computer science degree. Be a woman pioneer in this new field. There are lots of jobs for computer science majors. Parents are lukewarm with this idea. Phew, glad that is settled! Computer Science it is. Everything is groovy… for now.

You guessed it, 20 credit hours later, I discovered that being a programmer was not my idea of a good time. Programmers weren't my people. My people formed Tribes. My people were hanging out at coffee houses, strumming guitars, discussing world problems and singing Kumbaya. My people had really long hair, wore tie dye clothes and spoke of making love not war. Programmers had pocket protectors and 4 function brick size TI calculators clipped to their belts. College Advisor sadly shakes his head. I drop out. I am lost. I need to find myself. I'm a loser with no clear purpose.

I get an entry level job paying medical claims for an insurance company. I'm a 'Natural', and 'Talented' they say, and gave me the most demanding corporate accounts. You are 'Smart' and 'Management Material' they say. Too bad you can't get into management without a degree, they say. Bummer.

Desperate at this point to get a degree, any degree, back to Ohio State I go to complete a Bachelor of Science Degree in Insurance and Risk Management. Parents are happy. New husband is happier. The tribe is growing. Still strumming the guitar. Life is good. The roar is back for this woman.

Watch out management, here I come! I had to reinvent my career 5 times due to mergers, economic downturns, market shifts and new bosses to get to the top. The brass ring is the officer title, a seat at the table and a corner office on mahogany row. Didn't care how I got there. Just know that I am 'Some Body', a VIP, a member of the club when I do. I dress like them, talk like them, think like them, play the game like them. These are my new people, my new tribe.

I become them, a Director and Corporate Secretary of a Global 500 high tech company. I'm not strumming the guitar any longer. I'm chanting company mission statements to the thousands of people I'm hiring, bringing executive teams together and traveling all over the world. I am the good corporate citizen. I got the brass ring - until the industry went bust.

In 2000, I was 46 years old and took the rest of the year off naively believing that I would be reemployed at the top in no time. What a shock it was to learn that doors didn't automatically fly open and there weren't several positions to choose from. Wait a minute, I'm 'Some Body'. I'm highly marketable. I have a great resume, so why am I unemployed for 12 Months? This wasn't supposed to happen. I followed all the rules.

My days were spent networking, sending out resumes and still nothing. I wasn't me. I was them and there were hundreds of us all looking and all sounding exactly alike. I had buried my True Value, True Self and Transparency under the piles of success. Just like them.

I began to really question my worth. I was totally unprepared for the new rules for successful executive careers. Getting to the top was old school. The new brass ring was having a purposeful career, custom-designing a lifestyle and living my legacy. I found new people and tribes who were doing exactly that. Cool became cool again. Strip away the piles of success, keep what is really important, and showcase the best of 'the best of me'. Become a thought leader. Become uniquely me again. Start strumming the guitar again.

I found my purposeful career and established The Legacy Track. For the past 10 years, I've shown thousands of highly successful executives worldwide in their 40's, 50's and beyond, how to proactively manage their careers through any economy, competitive market, natural disaster, global situation or stage of life.

At the executive level, the days are gone when your company will develop or groom you for the next position. Winging your career is over. Those who passively rely on *Luck* and *Fate* are already finding their career stalled, stuck or prematurely finished. Gone are the days when the great resume, the Company Brand and being the Super Star Executive elevates your status. What is new is the rise of the Independent Executive and The Legacy Career.

THE OLD CAREER RULES GOT YOU HERE...

THE NEW RULES FOR EXECUTIVE CAREERS WILL GET YOU THERE....

- to be valued
- to find a purposeful career doing something that makes a difference
- to be paid fairly for your True Value
- to have career options no matter what the business climate
- to provide a good life for you and your loved ones
- to live your legacy, not just leave one

There are four T's to having a fulfilling Life and a successful Executive Career in today's Branded "Me" Economy: True Value, Transparency, Tribes and Talent. True Value sets the stage for discovering your life purpose and mission. Living your True Value makes transparency easy. Your Tribes, people who share the same values, purpose and mission will easily find you, follow you and support you when you need help. In return you pay forward and help them without any expectation of return. Your next project or position or career move will come from Tribe referrals for many years to come.

True Value is taking a deep inventory of what you love to do, do incredibly well and the situation in which you thrive. True Value is how you make a difference for the greater good, showcasing the best of you and your experience. True Value transforms you into a highly valued specialist and thought leader. You may find this is a very difficult process because of all the years you have spent doing just the opposite – where mastering everything was the way up the corporate ladder. You have become a generalist - just like them - and have lost sight of your True Value specialty.

There are five key parts to The New Rules for Executive Careers.

1. Invest in Yourself. Become *You Inc.* – a One Person Conglomerate:-
   a. Create a *You Inc.* Independent Executive Business Plan: You are a "consultant" or "freelancer" hired for 2 – 3 years for a project/problem tailor-made for your True Value.
   b. You make the decision: When your project is implemented or the problem fixed, you will either move on internally to another project/problem that is a perfect fit for you or you will be working for another company. The Choice is Yours.
   c. Learn Best Practices from your tribe: Executive Career Strategist, Life Coach, Leadership Coach, Personal Brand Expert and Social Media Expert.
   d. Customize those Best Practices to fit your

Life and Lifestyle Plan.

    e. Plan and invest the time throughout the year to leverage your True Value, Life Purpose and Career Plan.

2. Know your True Value and Life Purpose:-

    a. Discover your Life Purpose. What is it that you do so naturally, others see it as clear as day and come to you for help?

    b. Understand your True Value: Know What You Love to Do, What You Do Incredibly Well and the Environment/Situation in which you do your best work. Hint: You volunteer quickly to do these things. Work is Play.

    c. Understand your Career Derailers: What you Don't Like to Do even though You Do it Incredibly Well. Hint: You procrastinate doing these things and it drains you of time and energy.

    d. Your highest value is to be the specialist using your True Value and your Life Purpose 80% of the time and not a generalist where Career Derailers occupy 50% or more of your time.

3. Have a Life and Lifestyle Plan:-

    a. What is the life and lifestyle you want for this year, in 3 years, in 5 years, in 10 years from now? Where will you be living? What will you be doing? Most people spend more time planning their vacations than planning their lives and careers.

    b. Live the life of your choosing by

prioritizing time first for those things that bring you fun, happiness and peace including time for relationships, spiritual & personal growth, health and recreation.

c. Manage your energy, not your time. Start the day with a full tank of positive energy and monitor the withdrawals. Quickly recharge the batteries by walking around 5 minutes every hour. Quietly sit and breathe in/out to a count of 6 for 3 minutes. Listen to 15 minutes of meditation music. Keep a gratitude journal.

d. Learn to shift yourself in the moment, and also those around you, from stress to a positive state so that you make your best decisions.

e. Conduct a Life & Career Audit every 6 months. Pay attention to the early warning signs - those small changes in your life, job and environment that you tolerate now may become big career derailers.

4. Have a Legacy Career Plan that supports the Life and Lifestyle:-

a. Have a Career Plan built around your True Value and Life Purpose for your 40's & 50's so that you have the career you truly want on your terms and on your timetable. Wing it and your company controls your career.

b. Plan for actively retiring 3 times: at age 57, 63 and 70.

c. Prepare for changing jobs/assignments every 3 years. The time is even shorter for those in the C suite – CEO, COO, CPO, CTO.

    d. Let go, shed, delegate your Career Derailers to others. Keeping them makes your career vulnerable to unexpected and premature career end. Keeping them reduces your True Value and income potential.

    e. Be selfish: accept jobs/assignments where 80% of the job plays to your True Value. There is a strategic project perfect for your True Value that needs to be implemented fast or a critical problem that needs a fast fix.

    f. Increase your compensation and value by leveraging your Internet Thought Leader following and status.

5. Build Your Personal Brand to Build Your Value for Your Own Advantage:-

    a. Brand yourself around your True Value and Life Purpose to attract the jobs/assignments in which you excel and make a difference. This is much better than trying to sell yourself when unemployed.

    b. Have a True Value Resume writen to your future CEO boss around your True Value – how do you improve market share, top line revenue and profitability?

    c. Manage your Personal Brand and leverage Social Media to build your value. Those who use Social Media become known as Thought Leaders and attact companies to them. Those who don't, aren't.

    d. Use Social Media and your Tribes to look for your next job/assignment regularly and systematically. It takes 6 – 12 months to find the next perfect job/assignment of your choosing.

FINAL THOUGHTS...
LEAVE A LEGACY OR LIVE YOUR LEGACY?

Maybe you are scratching your head and asking yourself the same question my executive clients are asking, "What is really important?" The interesting thing about the answer is that it is never about money. It is always about happiness, relationships, following dreams and making a contribution that means something.

Most of us in our 20's and 30's are trying to build our legacy. In our 40's and beyond we are trying to leave one.

I've made it my mission to teach executives **The New Rules** *for Executive Careers* and to proactively be prepared for any situation that may impact their career, their health, their lives and their loved ones. It is my dream that executives with healthy careers in their 50's will establish their **Legacy Careers** now, find the meaningful work that they seek and continue to contribute and pay forward for many years to come.

ABOUT MARIE

Marie Guthrie has revitalized the careers of thousands of executives who find their careers stalled, stuck or prematurely finished. The unprepared are desperate to get their careers back on track given today's 18 – 24 months job tenure. The competition is fierce when new owners, new bosses and market shifts change the game every 3 years.

Interviewed by Fortune Magazine and The Financial Times of London, Marie Guthrie is a recognized futurist and the leading authority on executive careers. Her projects have achieved international best practice and case study recognition. In 2010 Marie released The New Rules for Executive Careers manifesto pioneering groundbreaking strategies for executive career success in the new Branded "Me" economy.

It is her dream that executives with healthy careers in their 40's & 50's will establish their legacy careers now, find the meaningful work that they seek and continue to contribute and pay forward for many years to come. Marie's Legacy Career System has shown thousands of executives how to proactively manage their careers in any economy, competitive market, natural disaster, global situation or stage of life.

Marie has over 20 years experience as a senior executive and consultant in the very exclusive world of the Global 500 - Hitachi, Thomson Reuters, Microsoft, Exxon Mobil, Nokia, JP Morgan Chase, Celanese, Lockheed Martin, Delta, IBM, McDonalds, Xerox, BNSF, Accenture and many more. She was one of the first women to be named an officer at Hitachi. Marie is an innovative business leader, accredited ICF coach and productivity consultant known for building employee capabilities needed to achieve personal and business goals.

For more about Marie Guthrie, visit http://www.marieguthrie.com/ or call 972.510.5587 or send an email to concierge@marieguthrie.com

CHAPTER 6

STRATEGY #1: FUEL YOUR TRANSFORMATION

BY DAWN ROBERTSON

This isn't the most fun thing to talk about – but I used to wake up itching and feeling horrible.

I had a severe case of eczema – and nothing could make it go away. It was on my hands, my legs, on my face and it was constant misery. I tried various doctors, who put me on crazy diets where I couldn't eat anything at all (or at least, that's how it felt), and nothing at all worked.

Naturally, I was tired a lot of the time. I thought it was a consequence of not sleeping. I was also overweight – and I had high cholesterol. I was told that my high cholesterol wasn't something I could do anything about – it was hereditary and that was that. Oh, and did I mention I was also anemic? And had a thyroid disorder? And had constant headaches? And I was only in my early twenties? Yes, life wasn't exactly 'a bowl of cherries'.

After spending years going through a host of diets and doctors, I didn't feel one bit better and the only place I lost weight was in my wallet - from all the so-called experts that really did nothing for me.

Now, don't get too depressed, because this story *does* have a happy ending. I just had to tell you how bad it was so you can understand how good it became. Four years ago, I heard famed motivational speaker Tony Robbins interview Dr. Robert Young, author of "The pH Miracle for Weight Loss."

Dr. Young's belief is that humans hang on to too much acid in our bodies and they have to work hard to overcome this acidity. When you balance your internal pH, just like you'd do with a swimming pool, you'd lose weight, gain energy and transform your life.

Well, again, I'd been through the mill – and this could have been just another doctor with another method that wouldn't work for me. But this time, what Dr. Young was saying really resonated with me. I decided to give it a try - and this time I hit the jackpot. This may sound like a bad infomercial, but I literally could not believe the results.

Within two weeks, I turned around my health problems. The eczema went away. <u>My energy levels skyrocketed.</u> The doctor looked at my blood work and said my numbers were the best in his practice. Within four months, I dropped the excess weight and at 40 years old, I weigh the same as I did in high school.

I was achieving more. I felt so much better. And I was inspired to pursue a PhD in nutrition. I also became a personal trainer, quit my job and opened a women's gym.

For me, it was a miracle that I want to share. If you truly want to transform your life, first you must have the health and the energy to do it. It's what propels super-achievers like Tony Robbins and ultra marathoner Stu Mittleman – and it could do the same for you!

PH – TWO LETTERS THAT CAN CHANGE YOUR LIFE

As I mentioned earlier, the goal is to balance the pH of the body – to be exact, you want to maintain a pH of 7.365. When we eat more acid-forming foods rather than alkaline-forming foods, the over-acidification of our bodies results in fatigue. Regulating your pH balance, however, enables you to:

- boost energy levels
- increase strength and stamina
- increase mental clarity
- create a stronger immune system, and
- lose weight

That's exactly what it did for me.

The problem is that the foods we eat leave either an alkaline ash in our bodies – or an acidic ash. It depends on what kinds of foods they are. When it's a food that leaves an acidic ash, our bodies use up a great deal of energy just to eliminate it. If it is an alkaline ash, it's not such a chore for our body to get rid of it – which leaves us with an abundance of energy to spare. Depending on how we eat, our bodies are either in a high-energy alkaline state or a low-energy acidic state.

That acidic state comes largely from processed foods and animal products (both meat and dairy), including flour and sugar products, sweets, alcohol, coffee and artificial sweeteners. They take away both nutrients and energy from us.

How to gain those nutrients and energy back? With "live" foods, such as vegetables, sprouted grains, nuts, seeds, and fruits like avocados, grapefruit, lemons, limes, and tomatoes. If the food you eat doesn't add energy to your physical mix, it takes away energy instead – making you feel tired and lethargic. Broccoli can energize you. A bag of chips will *de*-energize you.

You can actually measure the energy in food, believe it or not. A hamburger contains about 5 megahertz of energy, while an avocado usually has around 120 megahertz. How does that relate to your body? Well, healthy cells vibrate at around 70 megahertz, sickly cells at around 50 to 60 megahertz and cancer cells at roughly 30. The amount of energy in the foods of your diet goes hand-in-hand with the energy levels you experience as you go about your day.

It only makes sense that foods which sit on a supermarket shelf for 6 months will have a lot less natural energy in them than something that was recently alive, such as a veggie that you grew in your backyard. The fact is that the further a food is from its natural state, the less energy it has – and cooking is a large contributor to that negative process. The more you cook food, the more energy it loses – while the more raw, green vegetables you put into your body, the stronger the powerhouse you build within yourself.

You can be more productive than you ever thought possible by avoiding low energy foods. On the flip side, fatigue plagues your body if it's too acidic. An acidic body is the perfect home for a host of toxic microscopic organisms, called microforms, and their poisonous excretions, known as mycotoxins. The microforms that grow inside an acidic body ferment the sugar that we would otherwise use for energy. These toxins that thrive in an acidic body reduce the absorption of nutrients such as protein and minerals. They also weaken energy production in the body.

Mycotoxins reduce strength and stamina, cause excessive fatigue, 'cloud' thinking and block ambition. They also deplete B vitamins, iron, and other minerals, which alone would cause someone to have low energy levels. In addition, they affect the pancreas, liver, and adrenal glands, which play major roles in controlling energy levels. Our electrolyte balance, which is necessary for cell activity, is also disrupted. They destroy essential enzymes, reducing cell energy; they also create oxygen deprivation in the tissues.

Yes, it all sounds pretty frightening. That's why the change I felt in my own energy, once I adjusted my diet and lifestyle, felt so profound. You can experience that kind of dynamic change yourself – so let me share my secrets to fueling your own personal transformation.

THE 7 STEPS TO YOUR OWN TRANSFORMATION

Step 1: Reduce Sugar and Refined Foods

The standard American diet uses sugar as a primary source of energy – but it's a quick fix that does nothing for you long-term. False energy sources such as coffee and energy drinks are obviously big business – but those, as well as refined foods such as pastas, breads and sweets, will lower your energy, not boost it. We end up quickly exhausting sugar energy, causing us to crash.

When you take the sugar out of your diet, however, your body begins to rely on fat as its energy source instead. Your body is far better off burning fat, because you tap into a virtually unlimited energy source. Fat is your body's fuel of choice because it is inexhaustible. The body can store about 160,000 total calories, with about 2500 of those being sugar. About 135,000 are from fat. When you look at those numbers, it's easy to see how sugar is just an "easy high" that gets depleted quickly. Eating sugar may give you a false sense of energy for the moment, but it will be followed by a large drop in energy levels, affecting your ability to focus and perform at your maximum potential. Sugar also creates acid, which makes our bodies use up even more energy trying to eliminate it, physically creating a "fatigue cycle" in our day-to-day lives.

Step 2: Introduce Alkaline-Forming Foods into Your Diet.

Alkaline-forming foods include *all* vegetables, with a special focus on raw, green veggies and low-sugar fruits such as avocados, tomatoes, lemons, limes, and grapefruit, as well as nuts, seeds, tofu and soybeans. Green foods contain chlorophyll, which has the ability to regenerate our bodies at a molecular and cellular level. Chlorophyll also helps your red blood cells carry oxygen throughout the body.

These kinds of raw foods contain energy, which is transmitted directly into your body. Of these foods, vegetables should make up the largest part of your diet. They are the most nutrient dense foods available – they also help protect against microform overgrowth and help neutralize acids in the blood and tissues. Ideally, 70% of our plates should be covered with vegetables. Our bodies are 70% water, so it makes sense we should feed our bodies with the same percentage of foods high in water content.

Step 3: Drink Water

As we just noted, water is the largest ingredient of our bodies – it's also the basis for all cellular and bodily functions. A decrease in your water intake affects the efficiency of all cellular activity. Losing *only 2%* of your body's water can cause you to lose energy and mental focus. Water also removes toxins from your system.

To properly maintain your health and energy, you should apply the following formula: Divide your body weight by half, change the pounds to ounces, and drink that quantity daily. In other words, a 180 pound man should be drinking a minimum of 90 ounces of water per day.

If you exercise, are overweight, or have chronic health issues, however, you should be drinking 3/4 of your body's weight converted to ounces. For example, that 180 pound man would now be drinking 120 ounces of water a day.

Beverages such as coffee (700 times more acidic than water) and soda (about *50,000* times more acidic than water) are toxic to the body. Not only will they actually dehydrate it, but the caffeine can impact your health in a variety of negative ways. The false sense of energy you get from caffeine and sugar is actually your body rushing to expunge the poison from your system. When your body uses up all of its energy to rid itself of that poison, you have little energy left for the things you want to do.

Step 4: Consume Plenty of *Good* Fats

Maybe you didn't know there was such as thing as "good" fat, but fats in the natural form provided in such foods as almonds, avocados, fish oil, and flax seed oil raise our metabolism to create more energy. These essential fatty acids bind with and eliminate toxins from our system and allow our bodies to use them for cellular energy. If you are overweight, cutting the good fats out of your diet will *not* help you to lose weight. Instead, you should severely limit processed fats and oils. You need to *eat* fat in order to burn fat – the right kind of fat. About 20% of your calories should come from fat.

Step 5: Avoid All Dairy

Despite what the dairy industry has brainwashed us to believe, dairy products are *not* healthy. Cows are injected with bovine growth hormone for the sole reason of increasing the production of milk for profit. In addition, we are the only species on the planet that drinks milk past infancy – *and* the only one that drinks the milk of another species. Instead, substitute almond milk or rice milk. Dairy products are extremely counter-productive, causing the body to use up energy to eliminate the toxins they create. If you want to see changes in your energy, weight, complexion and total health – give up *all* dairy in your diet.

Step 6: Eat 5 to 6 Small Meals a Day

Frequent meals help maintain high energy levels by regulating blood sugar and insulin levels. That means no more mid-morning Starbucks runs or afternoon energy crashes. You will experience high, steady energy all day long. You must never allow yourself to become so hungry that the only way to satisfy yourself is by eating sugary foods that give you a quick burst of energy. This also goes for dependence on soda and coffee. Three larger meals a day is an artificial man-made construct. 5 to 6 smaller meals a day is a more natural way to sustain and maintain yourself.

Step 7: Exercise

The overall energy of your body depends on the health of your cells. The health of each of those cells, in turn, depends on receiving sufficient oxygen, which ultimately fuels your body. Oxygen is one of the best ways to alkalize your blood stream – and exercise is one of the best ways to get that oxygen into you. Movement doesn't take energy away from your body – it creates it. Exercise also accelerates the lymphatic process, eliminating acids and wastes through the skin.

These are the 7 steps I followed to transform my life. Follow them and I guarantee you will see a difference in every aspect of your life. It's a big lifestyle change, there's no question about it – but the rewards you will experience will more than make up for any inconvenience. Live life to the fullest – and feel the new energy your grateful body

will provide you as you pursue your dreams with everything you have to give.

ABOUT DAWN

Dawn Robertson is a highly sought-after expert in the field of health and fitness. As a personal trainer, nutritional consultant, and speaker, Dawn focuses on getting clients weight loss results that last. Being a fitness competitor herself, Dawn combines the secrets of bodybuilders and fitness models with her knowledge of nutrition to create a highly effective body transformation program.

Dawn founded **212 Nutrition**, a consulting company designed to get clients lasting results in as little as 12 weeks. Whether you are looking to transform the shape of your body, improve your health, or enhance your athletic performance, Dawn can help you achieve your goal.

Dawn holds undergraduate and graduate degrees in education, and is completing doctoral level studies in nutrition. She currently holds certifications as a personal trainer through the Aerobics and Fitness Association of America (AFAA), as a bootcamp instructor by the National Exercise and Sports Trainers Association (NESTA), and as a Nutritional Consultant through the Global Institute for Alternative Medicine.

She is a member of the National Association of Sports Nutrition and the American Association of Nutritional Consultants.

CHAPTER 7

PROVIDE VALUE TO YOUR VIRTUAL VILLAGE

BY LINDSAY DICKS

"He who wishes to secure the good of others has already secured his own."
~ *Confucius*

Marketing yourself and your business at this juncture is both incredibly easier and incredibly harder than it ever has been in history. And, ironically, the fact that it is so easy is what makes it so hard.

First – the easy part. The explosion of online marketing has made getting your name around the virtual universe simple and affordable. You can *tweet* a sales pitch, you can Facebook your friends with your latest offerings, and use SEO (Search Engine Optimization) techniques to put your website at the top of the Google search results pages.

The hard part? So can everyone else!

Old-school advertisers used to complain about being lost in the clutter of commercial breaks back in the day when the only screen we had to stare at belonged to the television. But that was nothing compared to today's overwhelming avalanche of information coming at us from all directions at all times – not that we don't incur and encourage that avalanche on a daily basis, by constantly checking our iPhones and iPads while listening to our iPods.

The solution? It's a very old-fashioned one for such new technology, but it comes down to this – give to get. Make yourself useful. *Offer value, not spam.*

Be a person, not a commodity. It's *the* high-impact way to ignite your business and transform your world.

At CelebritySites, it's up to us to make our clients stand out in the overcrowded online world – and, more importantly, find the most powerful and innovative ways to *connect* them to their potential clients and customers. The first step to doing that is understanding that Twitter, Facebook, LinkedIn, etc. are only delivery mechanisms; the important thing to consider is this – *are you actually delivering anything of substance?*

BEYOND SIMPLE SELLING

Big corporations know better than anyone how hard it is to make a connection with today's consumer. That's one of the big reasons they now engage so heavily in what's called

"Cause Marketing," where they'll do a large high-profile campaign to benefit a nonprofit cause or charity. When a giant company is placing ads for charitable endeavors, they're not just doing it to be nice. They also know that it's good business.

53% of consumers say that if they have a choice between buying from a company they view as altruistic and one that they don't, they'll pick the altruistic candidate, according to a 2010 international study on Cause Marketing done by MediaLab. When over half of your customers say something impacts their choices that much, you listen. And that's why, currently, over 25 billion dollars is spent by companies all over the world, companies like Starbucks, McDonalds, Target and Home Depot, on Cause Marketing, which has increased by 220% over the past ten years, according to a 2010 MediaLab study.

Cause Marketing is the best way for a huge company to go beyond conventional advertising – and it's more and more necessary for them to get noticed, to improve people's perceptions, and to influence a consumer's buying habits. And, fortunately, it also helps a lot of worthwhile causes!

What does this have to do with all you entrepreneurs out there? It demonstrates that the biggest and best companies in the world know that in order to connect with today's marketplace, you have to go beyond a sales-only marketing mentality.

When we check our email in-box and see spam after spam, we just hit the delete button without even opening them up – we know those emails are just trying to sell us something that we really don't need or want. Your potential customers are no different. Unless you're offering something of possible value to them, they don't really want to spare even a moment to listen to your pitch – because most of the time, they are living hectic lives that leave them feeling like they don't have that moment to spare.

The goal is to make that moment worth it to them in whatever way possible.

PROVIDING PROSPECTS WITH VALUE

Door-to-door salesmen used to stick their foot in the door to prevent the homeowner from slamming the door in their faces. Today, more than ever, entrepreneurs need their own virtual version of sticking their foot in the door – so they can at least begin the conversation that can lead to a potential sale or even a new long-term customer or client.

There are several ways we help our clients deliver the kind of value that will enable them to make that all-important first connection. Here's a rundown of some of them:

PROVIDE FREE INFORMATION

Everyone wants something for nothing – and, if you want to reach prospects who are likely to buy what you're selling, a great way to do that is to offer free information in your area of expertise. This can take the form of a special free report that can be downloaded off your website (in return for the prospect's contact info) or an article that's syndicated on various online sites.

Once the report is created, you can advertise its availability through your social media outlets. Again, you're not overtly selling a product or service – you're offering free content that *ties into* what you're selling. You're starting the conversation and creating trust in you as an expert and authority in your field – which, in turn, makes them more comfortable buying from you.

PROVIDE FREE ADVICE

Again, before someone buys from you, achieving a certain comfort level is critical. While free information is important since it demonstrates you know the facts about your field, offering free *advice* shows you've got the experience and the savvy to help your clients achieve their goals. This advice can be distributed in a similar fashion to your free information – in the form of articles, special reports, etc.

For instance, if someone is thinking about buying a foreclosed house as an investment, and you put out a tweet that says:- Free report on: 'What to Avoid with Foreclosure Purchases', that person has everything to gain and nothing to lose by clicking on the link, getting that report, and giving them your contact information.

Another more direct way to provide free advice is a lot more time consuming, but also a lot more effective – by offering a free ten or twenty minute phone consultation or online chat, you give your prospect a one-on-one taste of who you are and what you're all about – but you don't give them enough to enable them to do what you do without you.

In line with that, providing free advice, and even free information, scares a lot of entrepreneurs – you might be thinking right now that by giving away your secrets, you'll be giving away your business. The important thing to realize is that most people don't have the expertise or experience to do what you do – and it's important to demonstrate that *you're good at what you're do* in order to overcome any buyer's resistance. Don't worry about sharing secrets – remember, you have to give to get!

THE PERSONAL TOUCH

It's generally much easier for an entrepreneur to employ "the personal touch" than it is for a large corporation – usually; the entrepreneur is at the center of their business, as opposed to a big impersonal company that might be lacking a central public "face." When you share your personality, your interests, stories about your family, your friends or even your pets, you show that you're a *person* that people can relate to.

Earlier, I said it was important to be a person and not just a commodity - this is where you can take that concept and put it into action. The best place to begin is with a personal blog and social media sites such as Facebook. You can write about business and personal challenges, funny stories that happen to you, or other events in your life. You can also cheer on other friends, recommend other entrepreneurs' services, or review a new movie or TV show you really liked.

Be positive and upbeat and don't limit yourself to your own sites and pages – comment on other Facebook friends' statuses and blogs, especially if they're posting something that's relevant to your business. Get *their* friends curious about who you are and what you do. The last thing you want to do is create your own virtual bubble – there's a big danger that you could end up talking to yourself. That's why, at CelebritySites, we make sure to get our clients' word out online everywhere we can.

SHOW, DON'T TELL

Video is fast becoming the preferred online method of communication. Many people aren't real enthusiastic about having to read – it feels too much like school. If they can just click on "Play" and watch something, they'll choose that option every time.

That means that if you can make a simple interesting video, with either you talking on-camera, or with bullet point information and visuals to match, you're giving your prospects a "show" they can watch. If you do put yourself on camera, you also become a real person to them – they can see and hear you and you're suddenly no longer a complete stranger.

Video enables you to make a vital connection faster – and again, you can share free advice and information in your field. Another advantage of video? By using it on your website, you keep visitors there longer, which improves your Google search ranking.

CAUSE MARKETING

Let's end with the idea we began with, Cause Marketing – because if it's good enough for a huge multinational corporation, it's good enough for you.

It's easy enough to offer a benefit to a popular cause and simultaneously link it into your business. For example, a dental practice could run a casino night to benefit a local charity or high school – and, at the same time, gather lots of new contacts to market to. The charity benefits and so does the practice.

On a smaller scale, you can sponsor a runner in a charity run or just simply link to your favorite cause on your website and promote it. You can even offer your particular product or service to a charity at no cost for their own fundraising purposes, and then ask for an endorsement after the fact.

Both of these local options give you plenty of opportunity to talk online about your charity involvement and, again, help others to see that you are more than just another marketer. But if you really want to help a cause in a more high-profile way, you can start a cause-oriented website that's relevant to, but separate from, your business.

For example, we have a client that is a personal injury lawyer. He started an entire campaign devoted to helping teens take the pledge not to text on their cell phones while they're driving. It's not only been a tremendous success, but it's also been an incredible force for good; while, at the same time, it shows that he's about more than just 'car accident' cases.

People buy people – and, at CelebritySites, that's exactly how we market our clients. One half of that effort is making sure we're up-to-date with the latest online tools and technology, as well as the most popular social media sites. The other half is making sure that the right content is there to effectively use that technology.

No one wants to see 500 tweets from someone with constant links to product pages… No one wants to be constantly "sold" – marketing is too pervasive in the 21st century and everyone already feels a little under assault. You can't make the right connection unless you add the right value to your sales equation – and without the right connection, you can't successfully market.

In today's "virtual village," the smart entrepreneur makes sure to become a contributing member of the online community. Provide value to your prospects – and that value will be returned many times over back to you.

ABOUT LINDSAY

Lindsay Dicks helps her clients tell their stories in the online world. Being brought up around a family of marketers, but a product of Generation Y, Lindsay naturally gravitated to the new world of content marketing. Lindsay began freelance writing in 2000 and soon after launched her own PR firm that thrived by offering an in-your-face "Guaranteed PR" that was one of the first of its type in the nation.

Lindsay's new media career is centered on her philosophy that "people buy people." Her goal is to help her clients build a relationship with their prospects and customers. Once that relationship is built and they learn to trust them as the expert in their field then they will do business with them. Using Social Media and Search Engine Optimization, Lindsay takes that concept and builds upon it by working with her clients to create online "buzz" about them to convey their business and personal story. Lindsay's clientele spans the entire business map and range from doctors and small business owners to Inc 500 CEOs.

Lindsay is a graduate of the University of Florida with a Bachelors Degree in Marketing. She is the CEO of CelebritySites™, an content marketing company specializing in social media and online personal branding. Lindsay is also co-author of the best-selling books, "Big Ideas for Your Business" and "Shift Happens," as well as the best-selling book "Power Principles for Success" with Brian Tracy. She was also selected as one of America's PremierExperts™ and has been quoted in Newsweek, the Wall Street Journal and USA Today, as well as featured on NBC, ABC, FOX and CBS television affiliates speaking on social media, search engine optimization and making more money online.

You can connect with Lindsay at:

Lindsay@CelebritySites.com
www.twitter.com/LindsayMDicks
www.facebook.com/LindsayDicks

CHAPTER 8

CHANGE YOUR BUSINESS – CHANGE YOUR LIFE

BY RICHARD SEPPALA

"They must often change, who would be constant in happiness or wisdom."
~ Confucius

For most of us grown-ups, our work takes up the majority of our waking hours – (unless you really are one of those guys on the internet who supposedly made a million dollars in their pajamas – or does the pajamas thing mean they also work while they sleep?) This goes double (or triple, or quadruple…) when you run your own business.

That often means that, as our businesses go, so go our lives. The two are intertwined to the point that you're often on your iPhone checking email or making calls while you're watching your kid play soccer.

Of course, if your business is doing well, if you have systems in place that relieve some of the stress of managing things, if you are in charge of your own company... it allows you enough money and freedom to properly enjoy your family and your friends, to travel and to pursue other outside interests.

On the other hand, if your business weighs you down at every turn – you're not making enough, you have to micro-manage everything, you're not generating enough new customers or clients and every day is a struggle to stay afloat – that too colors all other aspects of your life. You battle with stress and fatigue and that affects you and everyone around you.

I'm not one of those people that preaches that your work shouldn't be important. Running a business and running it well is crucial to building the kind of life you want – and a good example to your children, if you have them.

I do believe, however, that running your business from a negative place is unproductive and harmful to your overall life and health. If you follow old and ineffective patterns that continually make you unhappy and don't take your business to where it needs to be, change is absolutely necessary. Otherwise, it becomes almost a form of self-punishment – which, unless you're into that sort of thing, quickly takes a toll.

There are always periods of high stress and long work hours when you're running your own business – it can't be avoided, especially when you're still in the building phase. But if you see no actual light at the end of the tunnel, if more stress and more working hours just breeds *more* stress and *more* working hours, it's time to think differently.

Too many of us get stuck in ruts and become afraid to take a chance on solutions that could not only make us happier and more content, but also the people we know. Well, a few years ago, I took that kind of chance. But it wasn't because I'm particularly courageous. Actually, I didn't really feel like I had a choice.

MY TRANSFORMATION

I started out in the corporate world – and worked my way up to being responsible for sales and marketing for some of the biggest senior companies in America. Naturally, this resulted in an overwhelming amount of constant travel to the various senior communities across the country.

But my personal life had a very big wrinkle to it – I found myself in the position of single dad, raising my new son, Cole. And suddenly, all the travel that was necessary to being able to do my job was a huge problem. That problem hit the crisis point when Cole developed separation anxiety when I was gone – and that anxiety became so severe, he ended up being hospitalized for it.

That's the point where everything had to change for me - there was no question about it. I immediately resigned from my position, because my son was obviously more important than any job could be.

Up until that day, I had never considered running my own business – but now, I needed to figure out a way to make money without leaving town. In other words, just as the title of this book reads, I totally had to *ignite my business and transform my world* – which meant looking at my experience and my skill set in a way I never had before.

I realized that at the corporate level, I had learned a lot of marketing systems and techniques that traditionally *stayed* at the corporate level. And that led to a breakthrough that propelled me into becoming the "ROI Guy" I am today.

What was behind that breakthrough? The fact that all those incredibly valuable marketing systems that the big companies depended on could be effectively used by *small* businesses in a way that could help level the playing field for them.

Yes, I could help the small guys operate like the big boys.

SOLVING THE THREE BIG PROBLEMS

I branded myself as "The ROI Guy," because I decided my focus would be on increasing the Return on Investment of marketing and advertising. I felt that what I had to offer small and medium-sized businesses in that area were the tools that could help them also 'ignite their businesses' in ways they had never thought of.

To begin with, many of them didn't really *think* of themselves as businesses.

Let's use, for example, a dentist – I'm married to one, so I know that drill (pun intended). A dentist goes to school basically to learn how to be a dentist – they're not after a business degree, even though they may take one or two courses in the subject.

Unfortunately, what they discover – as do many other professionals such as lawyers, doctors, financial services experts, etc. – is that *they are, in fact, businesspeople.* They have to be, because they *are* running their own businesses. They can't just worry about filling cavities – they have to be concerned with bringing in new patients, retaining current patients and putting in place the right kinds of sales and marketing systems - in which they usually have absolutely no training.

I began by offering a solution to what I saw as Big Problem #1. These kinds of professionals realize they have to do some kind of marketing – so they end up spending money on advertising that may or may not work. They have no way of knowing what's effective, unless a patient tells them they saw one of their ads in the paper. And that's anecdotal evidence that doesn't really mean anything.

The first service I knew would be important to these businesses would be a call tracking system. By assigning a different toll-free number to different marketing placements, they could instantly know which ad – and which ad message – received the most responses. That could help them focus on where to advertise and what to advertise – so they could generate the most leads for their outlay.

But that brought me to Big Problem #2. When the calls came in from these ads, they were frequently mishandled. Whether you're making sales calls or taking them, there is an art to handling a prospect so you make the sale or get them in for an appointment.

Unfortunately, most of these businesses had untrained receptionists or staffers taking these incoming sales calls. That meant they didn't volunteer information about the business that could make a difference. They often weren't even friendly. Worst of all, they either didn't get the contact information of the prospect who was calling or they wrote it down on a place where it was bound to get lost.

And frankly, this is a huge setback at most businesses where up to 75% of those kinds of calls get mishandled. You never know when someone who's calling could end up not only as a new customer, but a new lifetime customer. Figure out the lost total cash value of that person's business over a few decades, and you could end up 'banging your head against the wall' for a very, very long while.

I saw a two-pronged approach to solve Big Problem #2. One way was to begin offering sales training for those who answered the phones – I knew all the techniques from the time at my corporate job.

A second (and better) way was to set up a pre-recorded message where the prospect could leave their contact information. That way, even if the office was incredibly busy or off-hours, the staff, as well as the business owner, didn't have to worry about blowing an important incoming sales call.

Moreover, the pre-recorded message was set up to offer a "Call to Action" to motivate the caller to leave their info. That Call to Action would be an offer of free information, a free consultation or some other special deal that would require the prospect's contact details.

And that took me to Big Problem #3 - crucial contact information was still getting lost in the shuffle too many times, even though people were leaving it on a recorded message.

Please keep in mind that I don't mean to paint these businesses as being full of idiots who spend the day walking into doors. As I mentioned before, most of them are simply too busy working on their core business to deal with marketing. That's why I wanted to automate these processes as much as possible and make it easier for them.

The next step to doing that was to provide software that would *automatically* transcribe the messages from incoming lead calls – and *automatically* upload their contact information into a program that would store it for future marketing campaigns. No chance of anything getting lost. I called this package, "The ROI Bridge" – because it effortlessly bridged any possible gap in the marketing process.

All of this helped my clients eliminate wasteful spending on marketing that didn't work and also saved them from the day-to-day hassle of dealing with incoming sales calls when it was inconvenient. They could respond to them on their time and at their convenience in the most pro-active way. And it made a major part of their business, which made them uncomfortable, suddenly easy to deal with… as well as enabling them to implement their advertising in a much more powerful way.

THE MAKING OF THE MATRIX

That section heading, "The Making of The Matrix," doesn't mean we just took a left turn into a behind-the-scenes look at the Keanu Reeves movie trilogy blockbuster. No, "The ROI Matrix" is just the latest extension of the process I've described above.

One day, a client said to me, "Richard, it's great to know how many responses we're getting from our marketing. But how many of those generated leads actually end up spending money with us? Can we measure what the real ROI is of a marketing placement or advertisement?"

Well, that was a challenge no real ROI guy could turn away from. So we created "The ROI Matrix," where we not only measure the quantity of leads, but also the quality – so the business owner could answer the question, "How many calls were converted into cash sales?" As a matter of fact, we break down *all* the callers into various categories, so you can see who's a repeat caller, who's just trying to sell *you* something and who just had a question and never bought a thing.

From a business standpoint, it was a necessary step – because what you really want to know is, compared to what you're spending on your marketing, what are you making? *That* is your real ROI. If an advertisement is generating a lot of calls that are just a waste of time, you'll know that that particular response rate isn't really gaining you anything.

MAKING THE CHANGE

I'm happy I made the switch from the corporate world to being "The ROI Guy." I'm more in control of my destiny and, since my wife and I now have four more boys, I obviously need a lot more family time!

I'm also happy that I'm now able to deliver high-level marketing systems to smaller businesses that possibly would have never been able to take advantage of them otherwise. They showed courage by taking that step with me – and, they tell me, it's made an incredible different to their individual operations.

Taking a step is sometimes hard, especially when it's a big step. You sometimes are afraid you'll fall on your face. And, to be honest, sometimes you do. But if you never try to step up, you'll never know how high you can go.

Change your business and you change your life. If it's not working, fix it. If it is working, make it better. Keep growing and working towards higher goals. It's not always easy – but it always pays off in the end.

ABOUT RICHARD

Richard Seppala, also known as "The ROI Guy™," is a marketing expert, business consultant and best-selling author who helps companies maximize their profits by accurately measuring the ROI (Return on Investment) of their marketing efforts. His latest revolutionary tracking system, "The ROI Matrix," measures 'to the penny' just how much revenue each specific marketing placement generates for a client.

Richard founded his "ROI Guy" company in 2005. In addition to his acclaimed marketing tracking systems, called "The Holy Grail of Marketing," he also supplies businesses and medical practices with cutting-edge sales solutions designed to facilitate the conversion of generated leads to cash-paying customers.

By identifying marketing strengths and weakness, The ROI Guy™ is able to substantially boost his clients' bottom lines by eliminating wasteful spending on ineffective marketing, as well as leveraging advertising campaigns that prove the most profitable. By providing "all-in-one" automated systems that allow for the real-time tracking of each generated lead, a business can easily access valuable marketing data with just a few keystrokes.

Richard's marketing expertise is regularly sought out by the media, which he's shared on NBC, CBS, ABC and FOX affiliates, as well as in The Wall Street Journal, USA Today and Newsweek. He's also launched his own television show, "ROI TV," which features interviews with other top marketing specialists.

To learn more about Richard Seppala, The ROI Guy™, and how you can receive free special reports and other invaluable marketing information from one of the country's leading experts, visit www.YourROIGuy.com or call Toll-Free 1-800-647-1909.

CHAPTER 9

ALLOW WISDOM AND INTUITION TO AMPLIFY YOUR POWER

BY LINDA A.B. MILLER

T rue "Power of Purpose" manifests itself in various ways to create change, inspire evolution and evoke abundance – yet it all flows through one particular portal...

PEOPLE

Seems obvious, doesn't it? If everything is energy and we're all connected – then whatever the universe is putting out - it's using all of us as the transmitter. Many people, especially in these interesting and challenging times we're living in, feel helpless, alone and somewhat abandoned by whatever guides us all. I firmly believe they're simply not listening, tuning in, or watching. Or, most importantly, ...*feeling*.

My truth – my power of purpose - comes from *connecting* with others. My brother used to joke that my forehead had a permanent sign on it that reads, "Talk to me!" That's because I love people – and they are attracted to that like a magnet and drawn in. I love talking with people and tapping into their energy – then helping them *use* that energy to transform their lives, their social projects, or their business.

The diverse and exciting paths I've traveled throughout my one-of-a-kind life have brought me awesome experiences. It's as though combining those experiences and my natural creative and intuitive gifts enable me to serve those who seek out our services at the Hamptons Creative Group.

ENTERING MY CURRENT CHAPTER

As one of the first women allowed to work in the marketing department at the global investment bank Goldman, Sachs in the 1970's, I took real-world financial education and used it to fuel my business and publishing house over the next twenty-plus years. Fortunately that became an ongoing success story, which enabled me to sell it off at a substantial profit just a few years ago.

Having spent over three decades in the business world, I understand its allure, challenges, promises and limitations in a way that only someone who has successfully navigated its choppy and often dangerous waters can. But, after selling the publishing company, I knew it was time to change things up!

As I contemplated the decision and considered what to do with the next chapter of my life, I came to the conclusion that it was my destiny to fully tap into my ability to "read" people and assist them in finding their own truth, their own way. My friends and associates call me "queen of networking" – because I can and *do* help empower others to find their own light. I enjoy doing it – it's FUN for me – and it's also one way I like to give back to the world.

I commit myself to helping my clients tap into their own personal "power of purpose"; allowing them to uncover ways to facilitate their dreams and the tools with which to deliver those dreams right to their doorstep. It's been the key factor for both my personal and professional success over the years – and it's why I decided to focus on it in my current business. Now is the best time to apply that focus – because my real-world business success both informs and increases how I help my clients in a very tangible, practical way.

Here are three ways that I work with clients, which can help you to find your own "power of purpose":

- **Brand Alchemist** - I work with what's most exciting about a brand or company and help that to fully flower. Sometimes you're so close to your own work that you can't *really* see what makes it incredible – I help you open your eyes just a little wider...
- **Marketing Concierge** - I help you find the way to spread the word about your product, service or campaign – whether it's using the latest social media tools or recommending creative ways of

utilizing more conventional paths.
- **Connector** - I use my networking skills to connect you with others who can directly help support your project. If something's not in my skill set, odds are I know someone who is an expert at whatever your project requires. Someone once asked me if there was anyone I *didn't* know – my reply was, if there is, it's only because I haven't met them yet!

With several decades of business success behind me, I still approach my work with others on a very **intuitive** level. I trust my instincts and honor that intuition – because I believe in working *with* the flow, not against it. By tuning into and connecting with the process that enables serendipity and synchronicity to promote progress, you have much more than experience and expertise working in your favor – you have a universal creative power behind you, propelling you to the next level.

This is what gives any person or project an authentic strength that surpasses a simple strategic marketing plan. And it's what I rely on in my everyday life.

WISDOM NUGGETS

Much like my cherished friends or my favorite jewelry, I've acquired a number of "Wisdom Nuggets" over the years that are the foundation for how I work with people today. Life is a boomerang – and it brings back to us exactly what we put out there. That's why we all need to continue to put out the good stuff – because sometimes '*karma* ain't pretty'!

Always trust your process.

No one else knows what's right and what works for you. They don't know what's worked for you in the past and what will work for you in the future. Your intuition is always trying to tell you something – listen to that whisper in your ear, that flutter in your tummy, that pain in your neck - and you'll be rewarded!

Have patience and tolerance.

I'm sure you need no reminder that life often throws us a few curveballs, little setbacks and obstacles – and that some people aren't always honest. Look at who or what holds you back and learn from it. You'll be surprised to see how that process actually enables you to grow and become stronger.

Always speak your Truth.

Living an authentic life means that you sometimes come face to face with conflicts or challenges. But this allows you to gain more respect and authority from those around you. Show up for those moments fully, self-express and speak what's in your heart, even when it's hard to do. Modesty and discretion are sometimes called for, but too much compromise can leave you emotionally drained, diminished in spirit and without a confident voice. So speak up!

Work on your work ethic.

Yes, I talk a lot about intuition and process. But just as experience informs intuition, commitment to your work and passion projects makes things happen. You can't just expect success without putting in the time and effort –

money and recognition don't just fall from the sky. Applying the proper work ethic to the right process is an unbeatable combination for advancing your cause, your mission and yourself.

Listen and honor your intuition.

Malcolm Gladwell touches on this very subject in his book Blink. Going with your "gut instincts" isn't just a catch phrase. Your whole body is compiling information and sends signals out to you for a reason – sometimes to warn you off a bad situation and sometimes to spur you on to pursue an opportunity. When you go against your intuition, you're going against an important inner voice that's there to help guide you – and that leads to needless challenges that could reverse your course. Trust your gut and go with the flow of energy and intuition.

Be clear and ask the right questions.

Leaving a situation foggy and undefined can make that situation more challenging than it needs to be. Getting clear and finding out exactly what's needed and what the next steps are for you and others means everyone's moving in the same direction, toward the same goal – or at least, you'll be afforded the opportunity to uncover if someone isn't. Get the answers you need to find peace with what's at hand.

Always do what's best - next.

Start from where you are – and simply take the best next step, with the information you currently have at hand. It may not always seem like the smartest thing to do – as a matter of fact, it may feel like the downright dumbest thing to do – but if you proceed from the right place inside yourself, your steps will be readily apparent and, ultimately, lead you to the best destination for yourself.

Take responsibility for your actions.

It's easy to blame and point fingers when we believe a mistake has been made. But it's also disruptive and toxic to the harmony of any healthy enterprise. Be accountable for your actions – and be kind to others who admit their shortcomings. We are all too human – and we need to support one another in moving forward. There's power in passion, not in seeking perfection.

Keep your self-respect...

That old saying we teach other's how to treat us is true - if you don't respect yourself, others will follow your lead. Back up your beliefs with actions, speak truthfully and don't allow others to tear you down. Be a shining and brilliant example of personal strength, commitment and self-respect.

...and respect others at all times.

The other side of that coin is also showing others that same respect – reflecting it back at them even when they honestly disagree with you about something. By respecting others and demonstrating it in your everyday life, you again show your personal strength and willingness to trust the process of others as well as your own.

So this isn't the usual get-rich-quick advice you'll get from most business gurus! I believe building a firm foundation on these "Wisdom Nuggets" reaps you far more rewards in the long run - as well as allows you a large measure of personal satisfaction!

WRITING YOUR SUCCESS STORY

I've put a lot of emphasis here on personal integrity and doing the right thing – because it's incredibly important to me. Helping you write *your own* success story is incredibly important when you're my client – after all, it *is* what you hired me to do!

So I'd like to share with you a bit of my process for helping my clients reach their desired destination of achievement and accomplishment:

1) What's the real story?

My ability to connect with people also enables me to uncover their real story, even if they can't quite express it in words. As I noted earlier, some people miss the big story when it comes to their own brand – but since my intuition plays such a large role in our team's approach, we are able to reflect back at them their own amazing, authentic, brand story.

2) Brainstorm and strategize.

Next, we want to get the creative juices flowing in order to build a compelling theme around which the client can tell their story. In many cases, that story has never been properly told – or even told at all! We don't like to hide in the past – and we like to face the future head on. Therefore, we encourage clients to raise the bar on their own expectations and walk towards their own light.

3) The toolkit.

Today, we have an amazing array of tools at our disposal to market that story and the theme we've built around it. We love all the fabulous new media and marketing opportunities – such as Facebook, Twitter, blogs, etc. – because of their immediacy and grassroots "oomph." At the same time, we recognize the power and effectiveness of traditional marketing methods, and apply them as they make sense for each particular client's story.

4) Connecting the dots.

Through this process, we always do everything we can to maintain the "personal touch" with clients. In this fast paced era of sexy technology and instant communication, we still love a handwritten note, a handshake, a face-to-face meeting, whatever it takes to make sure we're "in synch" as people and not just as business associates.

Having been on the client side of creative agencies for many years, I've seen and understand that, while technology has improved the number of ways which client and agency can communicate with one another, it can also distance that relationship and, in some cases, inhibit the collaborative process.

People are the power behind our purpose – the critical element that we don't allow to get lost from our winning equation. Remember to rise above the dollars and cents in your business dealings and connect with the people involved.

Passion, purpose and connecting with other people helps us all share in our greatest successes. Grab life by the hand, don't take every challenge so seriously and remember it's a dance! It doesn't have to be difficult – the challenges of dancing in the flow of the moment are what help each of us grow, stretch, meet new friends and colleagues and uncover our greatest and most unique gifts. Celebrate today and say "YES" to your fabulous future!

ABOUT LINDA

Linda A.B. Miller is a true connector, collaborator and marketing concierge. As a Brand Alchemist, Linda helps her clients synthesize their ideas and turn their brands into gold. Experience, strength and hope are the core values that drive Linda's thoughts, actions and deeds, which are the secret sauce for her success in business, the community and her relationships.

Linda founded Hamptons Creative Group after a 30 year career in publishing, investment banking, and fashion, (Linda was one of the first women to join Goldman Sachs' marketing team in the 1970's), which has allowed Linda's dynamic combination of business savvy and creative inspiration to position HCG as one of the most sought after marketing, advertising, and special events firms in the Hamptons and regional New York.

HCG's diverse client base thrives in partnership with solo-preneurs, retailers, charities, non-profits, and cultural and community leaders and is reflective of the value of HCG's creative solutions. Listening to and learning from a client's objectives to gain a thorough, intimate profile of target audiences, HCG's work is not only well-designed and flawlessly executed: it's vibrant, catalyzing work that speaks to audiences on a visceral, emotional, value-based level, and most important of all, increases the profitability, reach, and profile of a business.

Hamptons Creative Group is on a mission to serve its clients in bold new ways:

Linda's position as a highly visible female business owner offers clients key insights into some of the most coveted consumer segments (namely, luxury, entertainment & real estate). These segments can not only directly bolster a client's bottom line profits, but because of their close-knit community ties, often spread a business' message through 'word of mouth' and social engagement. Today, viral marketing activities are an essential part of any contemporary marketing strategy or advertising plan, but often elude businesses and agencies… precisely because these special consumer groups are so difficult to penetrate.

To further maximize the personal touch, HCG de-virtualizes the relationship between clients and agencies. "Having been on the client side of creative agencies for many years, I realized that while technology has improved the number of ways in which client and agency can communicate with one another, it's also distanced that relationship and, in some cases, inhibited the collaborative process. By founding our agency in the Hamptons, where our clients live, work and play, we can engage them, understand their challenges more deeply, and provide them with solutions that exceed their goals. And we can do it sitting across the table from one another."

Linda has a passion for old-fashioned marketing and networking, combined with the innovation of new media. To maximize the personal touch, Linda's mission is to de-virtualize the relationship between clients and agencies.

"Having been on the client side of creative agencies for many years, I realized that while technology has improved the number of ways which client and agency communicate with one another, it's also distanced that relationship, and in some cases, inhibited the collaborative process," she said.

Linda's position as a highly visible and pioneering woman entrepreneur offers her clients key insights into some of the most coveted consumer segments – entertainment, high end real estate, and fashion. These segments can not only bolster a client's bottom line profits, but because of their close-knit community ties, often rely on spreading an exclusive message through "word of mouth" and social engagement. Today, viral marketing activities are an essential part of any contemporary marketing strategy or advertising plan. But they often elude businesses and agencies, precisely because these special consumer groups are so difficult to break into.

Linda's secret sauce for success in her business and that of her clients is her ability to connect, open doors and act as a marketing concierge. As a Brand Alchemist, Linda helps her clients' synthesize their ideas and turn their brands into gold. Experience, strength and hope are the core values that drive Linda's thoughts, actions and deeds, and her signature for success in business, community and relationships.

CHAPTER 10

LIVE ON PURPOSE

BY VIVIAN BERNARDO

"Wealth -- the ability to fully experience Life."[1]

A re you wealthy? Or are you captive in the "rat race"? The *rat race* is defined as an endless, self-defeating pursuit (Webster's dictionary). The *rat race* conjures up images of the futile efforts of the rat attempting its escape from a maze or the wheel. I was stuck in that maze for 15 years. In the next few pages, I will share the vision which fueled my escape from the *rat race*.

Growing up in Los Angeles, I witnessed my parents trapped in this *rat race*, living ordinary, complacent lives. They came to America in December 1972 to live the American Dream. I was only 11 months old. I grew up in humble beginnings. My parents were first generation, traditional, hardworking individuals working 40-60 hours per week for somebody else in the retail industry. They struggled, living paycheck to paycheck. Sound familiar? There was always too much month at the end of the paycheck. Tension was palpable, particularly when it came time to pay the bills which inevitably led to a shouting match.

My parents worked tirelessly in this *rat race* which became their daily existence. Every morning, during the work week, they reluctantly woke up to the alarm clock. They made breakfast, packed their lunches then drove me to school and the babysitter. After a hard day's work, the cycle does not end. Dinner had to be made and the vegetable garden watered. Then they watched TV for a couple of hours before retiring to bed just to do it all over again the next day! They counted the days until Friday. "Thank God it's Friday" was a common phrase in our household. For the most part, the weekend consisted of chores, gardening, church, fast food restaurants, and grocery shopping and perhaps visiting with family or friends. The weekends were never long enough. I recall every Sunday evening, my dad would always lament… "work, work, work again!"

Growing up in a traditional household, my parents emphasized the value of intellectual pursuit. My parents' desire was for me to become a doctor. They constantly reminded me to study hard, get good grades. Hence, becoming a stellar student became my singular focus. My entrepreneurial friends always told me I had so much "book smarts" but no "street smarts"! At the time, I never understood what they meant. My beliefs were similar to those of my parents, that a college, masters or professional degree is the foundation for a secure future.

As I grew older, it became increasingly evident that my parents' entire existence revolved around me, their only child. It was a blessing for me, yet a sad reality for them. I vividly recall my parents' wishful thinking that they would travel the world… "someday"; that "someday" never came. Today, my Mom is no longer with us. Sadly, she succumbed to leukemia at the very young age of 58. At the time of her diagnosis, she was a picture of health – vibrant, dynamic and a social butterfly.

During her bout with cancer, my father decided to take an early retirement from his job to be with my Mom, his wife, his best friend. I made a conscious decision to put my dream on hold. I was contemplating medical school with the intent of becoming an orthopedic surgeon. Finances became increasingly scarce. I knew I had to make a living for my father and me.

I found myself in Corp America. I was working for a Fortune 500 company within the telecom industry in Corporate Sales. It was the challenge and income potential that kept me in this position for over a decade! I learned invaluable life skills. I ultimately realized these were the "street smarts" I was missing. The top producer of the company was a professional surfer with no college degree. He basically had a positive "can-do" attitude, industry knowledge and life skills! My first year in this industry began the progressive shift in my mindset.

Fifteen years later, as the economy continues to shift, so does corporate America. Today, increased layoffs, less compensation, disgruntled employees are main stream in the corporate world. Tension is palpable. Stress is rampant. I have witnessed firsthand the negative effects of chronic stress within the workforce. I have a friend and former colleague who had been diagnosed with Stage 4 throat cancer. Fortunately, he is alive to share his story! His sheer willingness and vision to live made him a survivor! Today, he is no longer in corporate America. He is currently working for himself and genuinely living Life!

Financial insecurity has also plagued many of my peers. I recently had a conversation with a colleague who was still working just to make a living. He is 62! He lost a fortune in his savings plan! My friend's dad worked for the same company in the entertainment industry for 30 years only to find his retirement plan was insufficient to sustain his current lifestyle. Sadly, he and his wife are forced to reduce their standard of living.

So why did I stay in Corporate America for 15 years? Basically, I was comfortable. I was sold on the corporate plan. Work hard for a large corporation and invest into their savings plan. For the most part, the plan made sense until I lost 45% of the value due to a dip in the market! With the market instability and progressive inflation, I realized corporate America was not going to retire me. In my opinion, the 40-40-40 corporate plan is broken. Basically, working 40 hours a week for 40 years to retire on a meager 40% of my savings does not make financial sense! Yet, like many others, ignorance and fear kept me in the *rat race.*

"The entrepreneur in us sees opportunities everywhere we look, but many people see only problems everywhere they look."[2] In March 2007, my colleague introduced me to a wellness product distributed through network or referral marketing. Like many people, I was skeptical and negative. Out of respect, I decided to attend the opportunity meeting with my fiancé. The speakers were young and new to the business, yet these 20 year olds were earning $30,000 a month working less than 20 hours a week! He figured, "if they can do it, so can I!" At the time, my fiancé worked 60-80 hours a week as a project designer in an engineering firm. He invested in the opportunity on the spot. I, on the other hand, was not sold. Having graduated from college with a Biology degree, I had the false notion that I was smarter than most people in the industry and I was not going to rely on anyone for my success. My "book smarts" became a liability.

"Formal education will make you a living; self education will make you a fortune."[3] My fiancé was genuinely excited about the opportunity; hence, I kept an open mind and began my quest in personal development. I started attending trainings and seminars, listening to the mentors who have achieved industry success, reading books and listening to CD's. My car became a rolling university. Today, I am grateful for the self education, the life skills I have gained through network marketing. The "street smarts" my entrepreneurial friends were referring to, is applicable to all aspects of Life, in any industry, any business. Equally important, the journey has given me the opportunity to search within myself to discover the burning desire to live each day on purpose.

I am excited about the opportunity to inspire, mentor, support and be of service to the many people ready and willing to make the change in their lives forever. I never thought in my wildest imagination I would become a professional network marketer! Knowing what I know now through self education, I am excited about the infinite possibilities Life has to offer, outside the *rat race.*

Why network marketing? Network marketing exemplifies the ideology you have to give to get. The only way you can be successful in this industry is to help others achieve success. What a concept! A far cry from corporate America! Zig Ziglar said it best, "You can have everything you want in Life if you just help enough people get what they want."[4] As soon as the people in the industry embrace this leadership mentality, growth in yourself and in your business becomes inevitable.

Network marketing creates financial independence through passive and leveraged income. Personally, I love making money while I sleep, play or am on vacation! As an employee for a Fortune 500 company, the type of income I earned was linear income, income you earn when you exchange hours for dollars or in my case exchanging my productivity for dollars in the form of a sales commissions. In short, you do the work once and you get paid for it once. The disadvantage to linear income is if you stop work due to an illness or layoff, your income stops as in the case with my parents. Additionally, by exchanging hours for dollars, time is finite, therefore, no matter how great you are or your hourly rate is, your income potential is finite as in the case of my fiancé as a project designer.

The 2 types of income gained through network marketing is passive (also known as residual) income or leveraged income. In the case of residual income, you do the work once and you get paid over and over again. Examples include cash flow from rental properties or royalties for the work created by writers, inventors and singers. Leveraged income is income you earn through the efforts of others. Examples include franchising your business or hosting **a seminar** where *each* participant pays you a fee. John D. Rockefeller said it best, "I would rather have 1% of the efforts of a hundred people than 100% of my own."[5]

Why the wellness industry? As an entrepreneur, the wellness industry is poised to become the next trillion dollar sector of our economy. Today, everyone wants to be more healthy, fit and youthful. The target market is everyone.

As a personal mission, I have found meaning in inspiring others to fully experience Life – personally, physically and fiscally. As of 2009, the U.S. population reached 305 million (U.S. News). 2/3 of Americans are overweight; 1/3 is obese (Center for Disease Control); 1 in 3 adults suffer from hypertension (American Heart Association); 7.5% of children and adults suffer from diabetes (American Diabetes Association). An estimated 1.4 million new cases of cancer were diagnosed in 2008. Approximately 1 in 3 women and 1 in 2 men in the United States will develop cancer over their lifetime (American Cancer Society). America is losing the battle.

My mom did not have a second chance at life. Her dreams died with her. What are your dreams, your goals? What is your image of wealth? Wealth conjures up different images for different people. For me, wealth is all encompassing -- financial independence, time freedom, quality time with family and friends, luxury travel, ocean view estates, optimum sense of self worth, health and well-being. My daily living involves building and maintaining a personally, physically and 'fiscally fit' lifestyle for myself and for others.

"Network Marketing gives you the opportunity to face your fears, deal with them, overcome them, and bring out the WINNER that you have living inside of YOU!"[6] As an entrepreneur in the pursuit of my vision, I am inspired by the emotion, energy, and gratitude of the lives transformed everyday by this industry. Every day, I wake up energized by the power of purpose. I am devoted to something bigger than myself, a calling that gives new meaning to my life. The change was not overnight. My life is analogous to a marathon. When I decided to run the L.A. Marathon back in 2005, I had never run more than 3 miles. I committed to doing something each day to build my mindset and my body. I joined a team and hired a coach for support and guidance. Every Saturday morning, the team ran a few miles more than the previous Saturday. In a period of 6 months, we were running up to 25 miles! On March 3, 2005, I finished the L.A. Marathon (26.2 miles) in 5 hours and 28 minutes.

Figuratively speaking, my life, like the marathon, is "a journey of a thousand miles" which began "with a single step"[7]. First, I had to decide what I wanted out of life. I wrote down my short term and long term goals. I created a vision board. Most importantly, I took *action everyday*!

So where do you begin? "Begin with the end in mind."[8] Write in detail your image of wealth. Write down your goals. Become proactive, not reactive. Do a little everyday to get you one step closer to your goals, whether personal, physical or fiscal. It's the little things you do today that will matter most tomorrow. In the pursuit of your dreams, remember, "Success is a journey not a destination."[9] "Take the first step in faith. You don't have to see the full staircase, just take the first step."[10] Most importantly, "Never, never, never give up!"[11]

. . . .

Resources

1. Henry David Thoreau, American Essayist, Poet and Philosopher, 1817-1862

2. Michael Gerber, *The E-Myth,* Harper Collins, 1995

3. Jim Rohn, *Treasury of Quotes*, Jim Rohn International, 1994

4. Zig Ziglar, *Secrets of Closing the Sale*, McGraw-Hill, 1984

5. John D. Rockefeller, American Industrialist and Philanthropist, 1839-1937

6. Robert Kiyosaki, *The Business of the 21st Century*

7. Lao Tzu, Philosopher and Founder of Taoism

8. Stephen Covey, *The Seven Habits of Highly Effective People,* Free Press, 1990

9. Arthur Robert Ashe, Jr., *Off the Court*, Dutton Books, 1981

10. Martin Luther King, Jr., American Baptist Minister and Civil Rights Leader, 1929-1968

11. Sir Winston Churchill, *Never give in* speech, 1941

ABOUT VIVIAN

Vivian Bernardo is an entrepreneur at heart with a passion for helping others live life to their absolute fullest – personally, physically and fiscally. She is a personal empowerment advocate with a "can-do" attitude. Her mission in life is to contribute to the growth and positive transformation of as many people as possible - who are caught between their dreams and their day job.

She left her 15-year career in corporate America to pursue her passion. She has transitioned into the world of entrepreneurship in the field of network and internet marketing. She is committed to empower as many lives as possible by sharing her knowledge and experience. She is driven by the fact that she succeeds by helping others succeed.

As an Ambassador to the Millionaire Mind Training Program, she has helped hundreds in developing a winning mindset. As a coach in her industry, she strives daily to educate others on both the mindset and the system which has helped millions catapult their businesses to the next level.

Vivian is an active member of Women on Point, a women's networking group based in Orange County, CA, helping women achieve their goals personally and professionally.

Her long term vision is to help millions achieve personal empowerment, optimum health and financial independence; hence, the ability to fully experience life.

Vivian enjoys reading self development books, spending time with her family, running, hiking and traveling. She currently resides in CA with her fiancé, Waldemar (aka Val) and their 2 dogs, Chase and Zoe.

To learn more about Vivian Bernardo, visit www.vivianbernardo.com and www.twitter.com/CoachBernardo.

CHAPTER 11

THE HOLY GRAIL FOR SUCCESS

BY W. ROGER SALAM, THE CHAIRMAN & FOUNDER, THE WINNER'S CIRCLE INTERNATIONAL, INC.

- *What if there was **ONE** thing you could do to assure lifelong achievement?*
- *What if knowing this **ONE** code could unlock all your aspirations?*
- *What if unleashing this **ONE** idea could open the floodgate of success?*
- *(Hint: this **ONE** idea was used by Edison, Rockefeller & Gates)*
- *Would you be willing to apply this **ONE** principle?*

Well, there is such a principle. I know it's a bold statement, but this principle really can unlock the floodgate of success...and it's more effective than anything else you've seen. I wish I could take credit, but this practice was conceived long before my time. In actuality, it's a proven foundational principle of how to grow rich and become successful in virtually any endeavor in life, according to the father of the modern day personal development movement, Napoleon Hill.

The Mastermind Principle is powerful and investing your time in one will pay off in ways you never dreamt possible.

> *"None of us is as smart as all of us."*
> ~ *Japanese Proverb*

WHAT IS MASTERMIND?

Almost all of the great accomplishments and miraculous achievements of history were brought about through the power of this principle. Quite simply, Masterminding occurs when two or more individuals get together in the spirit of cooperative harmony to accomplish some goal, activity or result. It could be a common goal or their individual goals.

There is synergy of energy, commitment, and excitement that participants bring to a Mastermind Group. The beauty of Mastermind Groups is that participants raise the bar by challenging each other to create and implement goals, brainstorm ideas, and support each other with total honesty, respect and compassion. Mastermind participants act as catalysts for growth, devil's advocates and supportive colleagues.

Napoleon Hill in his timeless classic, *Think And Grow Rich* writes:

"Analyze the record of any man who has accumulated a great fortune, and many of those who have accumulated modest fortunes, and you will find that they have either consciously or unconsciously employed the "Mastermind" principle... Great power can be accumulated through no other principle!"

He continues ...

"No two minds ever come together without thereby creating a third, invisible intangible force, which may be likened to a third mind."

A Mastermind Group is formed when the group creates the agenda with their collective goals. Your peers give you feedback, help you brainstorm new ideas and possibilities, and set up accountability structures that keep you focused and on track. Each person's commitment and participation is vital.

The end result? Quite certainly, you will have created a community of supportive colleagues brainstorming together and moving the group to new heights. You'll gain tremendous insights to improve your business and personal life. Your Mastermind Group is like having your own personal and objective Board of Advisors.

THE HISTORY OF MASTERMINDING

One of America's most successful business tycoons, Andrew Carnegie, never got an MBA to learn how to run a business. He learned it from his own unofficial Mastermind group. At the age of 14, he got a job as a messenger boy for a telegraph company and saw all the messages from the local business barons. He found himself in a position to learn everyone's financial dealings, partnerships and business plans. By the age of 17, he had a complete business education, learning from those who were local successes.

Throughout his rise to the top, he continued to surround himself with those who knew more than he did. As part of the first official American business Mastermind group, the "Chicago 6", he swapped secrets with the founder of Wrigley's Chewing Gum, the owner of the Yellow Cab Company, the head of the world's largest ad agency, and other business titans. He also put the *Mastermind principle* in action with his own business management team.

In 1908, Carnegie commissioned Napoleon Hill to study the most successful people of their era and find out what qualities they possessed, or methodologies they employed, to become the leading businesspeople of their time. Out of that study came Hill's ground-breaking book, *Think Rich, Grow Rich*, which contained the 17 principles for supreme success. Carnegie was probably not surprised to see one of the three main foundation principles was Masterminding.

The surprising fact is that Carnegie was far from the first to come up with the idea. As of matter of fact, Masterminding was employed by one of America's founding fathers, Benjamin Franklin, who created what he termed a "club of mutual improvement" with local entrepreneurs. If you had any doubt that Masterminding brings forth big ideas, out of Franklin's group came the first library, paved streets, night watchmen and public hospitals.

Jesus, the Christian Messiah, used Masterminding. He personally selected twelve men and told them, "Follow me."

They did and the world has never been the same. Orville and Wilbur Wright did what was said to be impossible by building and flying the first airplane. Andrew Carnegie aggregated a team around him and built the world's biggest steel manufacturing company. Carnegie went on to become the first great philanthropist, funding over three thousand public libraries throughout the world. Likewise, Bill Gates and Paul Allen started Microsoft and became two of the richest men of all time and are now becoming two of the world's greatest living humanitarians.

The truth is Carnegie and Hill formalized a process that almost every successful person has employed throughout history – brainstorming with other great minds so that everyone can benefit from the combined talents and knowledge contained in the group.

MASTERMINDING YOUR WAY TO MILLIONS

It's been said that your income will be the average of your five closest friends. Not only is that is true for your income, but also holds true for your health, happiness, self-esteem, and just about every other facet of life – including mindset. When you keep company with successful people, their beliefs, habits and actions start to rub off on you.

I've made and lost multimillionaire status twice and this time I plan to keep it. I've made my share of mistakes and I believe that **"the only mistakes in life are those you never learn from."** As long as you learn from past mistakes, they are no longer mistakes, they are teachers.

As for myself, I became well acquainted with the power

of Mastermind and personal development in my early ca-reer, when I worked my way up to become the number one trainer and speaker for Tony Robbins. One of my pas-sions is to study successful people and find out what sepa-rates them from the rest. I've found that success is not an accident. In fact, successful people leave clues as to why they're successful.

Who you associate with and listen to will determine your destiny! Masterminding is all about associating and brain-storming with *only* successful people. Your struggles are not unique. Successful people have already gone through your struggles and know the shortcuts and the secrets to overcom-ing the odds and finding fortune.

If you'd like to become a millionaire, then rub shoulders with other millionaires. If you want to be an ideal parent, then spend time with people you believe to be model par-ents. Whether you want to 'save the whales', head-up an international empire, or run the most successful 'running shoe' store in east New Jersey; whatever it is you want, my personal philosophy is the same. It will happen faster, bet-ter, cheaper and stronger through Masterminding.

You learn from other's mistakes, which saves you time, money and helps you solve countless other problems. People who have gone before you share their experiences and you learn from their direct knowledge.

THE WINNERS' CIRCLE

In order to accelerate my own success, I started my own Mastermind group several years ago which started as a hobby and now **The Winners' Circle** has grown into one of the largest and most respected Mastermind group for speakers, authors, and information & internet marketers.

The Winners' Circle has been specifically designed to help entrepreneurs take their business to the next level through powerful and creative interactions with other high-powered successful professionals. This hand-selected mix of professional can provide the answers to virtually any business challenge. It's a private, invitation-only circle that isn't just about getting a few good ideas – it's about obtaining the tools to turbo-charge your business and eliminating the limitations you may have unconsciously placed on the success of your business.

We've taken the 20th century concept of Masterminding into the 21st century – call it Mastermind 2.0 – in order to give this already-powerful process more modern-day muscle.

"W. Roger Salam, aka "The Chairman" is the 21st Century Napoleon Hill. He mastered the Mastermind concept and took it to an entirely new level with his socially conscious advisory board model. His impact on entrepreneurship will be that of legends."
~Kelly O'Neil, CEO of Kelly O'Neil International and creator of Marketing to Millionaires™

THE MASTERMIND ADVANTAGE

There are many advantages of joining or creating your Mastermind group. Here are the (unfair) advantages our Winner's Circle members enjoy:

1. **ROI Focused Mastermind Group** – At The Winners' Circle (TWC), we don't just offer Mastermind. Our real product is your Return on Investment of time and money. Mastermind is just one of the ways we deliver ROI along with 17 other services to ensure and enhance members fulfillment.

2. **Synergy and Cooperation** – Cooperation, quite frankly, beats competition. When you work with others, you create a positive energy that's more than the sum of its parts. *The Winners' Circle is where 1 + 1 equals 11, not 2.*

3. **Specific Solutions to Challenges** – Rather than just hear bland advice like "Never Give Up" and "Hang in There," you've got experienced business people who have likely been in similar difficult situations you're currently experiencing. They know how they got through it and they can give you effective, meaningful action plans so you can, too.

4. **Increased Profitability** – Our Mastermind members are bottom-line oriented; otherwise they wouldn't be the successful people they are. They know the secrets to 'cutting the fat' and boosting sales.

5. **Cutting Edge Resources** – By gaining access to other business successes, you have access to the leading resources they use to build their companies and brands. This allows you to keep in touch with the latest trends and the newest profit-making tools available.

6. **Joint Ventures** - One of the most rewarding things to see is when two or more Mastermind members create a new business opportunity to make money for each other during a meeting. Expertise and experience often overlap in a

way that sparks new ideas and new partnerships in success.

7. **Accountability** – We encourage members to leverage the TWC 'law of accountability'. You are held accountable by others and motivated by peers. Most people will do more for others than they'll ever do for themselves. You dramatically increase your chances of reaching your goals when you have accountability partners.

8. **Camaraderie and Valuable Lifelong Friends** – Mastermind members inevitably bond as they share their own personal stories and strategies. You gain your own personal "board of directors" for your life and business – of which you are the chairman!

BOTTOM LINE

Everything good and great I have achieved in life, I attribute to Masterminding with like-minded successful people. To me, it's the most powerful step to take to get what you want in life. The fundamental idea behind The Winners' Circle is that "Success Breeds Success." Once more, whoever you listen to will determine your destiny. If you truly believe that, then why not surround yourself with "winners" by design and not by accident? Turns out, every single person inside TWC has been a hand- selected "winner" and worth listening to.

Someone once asked Helen Keller what was worse than not having sight. She wisely replied, "Having sight and no vision." Vision is not seeing something in a moment, but having the foresight to see what something can become, to see the possibility. Masterminding is all about seeing the possibility. Find a Mastermind Group that fits your needs or start your own, but don't wait to apply this most powerful principle to open the floodgates of success.

ABOUT ROGER

Roger Salam is The Chairman & founder of The Winner's Circle, the Largest & Most Respected Mastermind Forum for top Speakers, Successful Entrepreneurs, and Information & Internet Marketers. (www.JoinMyWinnersCircle.com)

Roger is currently the resident contributor and Financial Freedom mentor for "Yes, You Can Do It Club" a worldwide membership club for entrepreneurs with members from all seven continents that is growing through internet social networking (www.YesYouCanDoItClub.com).

Prior to getting involved in Real Estate investing, Roger served as a professional speaker and trainer with the world-renowned motivational speaker and peak performance coach Anthony Robbins. He has delivered over 3700 professional talks to various corporations, non-profit organizations and educational institutions in North America, Europe and Asia.

Roger Salam is co-author of two books on Marketing and "Secrets of the Real Estate Millionaires" and his latest book, "Mastermind Your Way to Millions" is due out soon. He's a graduate of UCLA, married to his high school sweetheart and has three lovely daughters. He is most passionate about sharing knowledge and resources and empowering people to reach financial freedom and higher levels of performance & success through the power of Mastermind!

The Winners' Circle International, Inc.
5831 Mariner St., Tampa, FL 33609
(813) 454-5999
support@TheWinnersCircleInc.com
For Free Bonus, Visit www.JoinMyWinnersCircleInc.com

CHAPTER 12

INTEGRATE, DON'T IMITATE

BY NICK NANTON, ESQ.

"Your only obligation in any lifetime is to be
true to yourself."
~ Richard Bach

What really ignites our passion for our business?

What fires up our ambition and causes us to make crucial decisions about what career paths we want to follow - and what level of success we want to attain?

Well, in many, many cases, it's *people* who initially inspire and motivate us in what we want to do with our lives – and how we want to do it.

People like Donald Trump. Richard Branson. Oprah Winfrey. These are people who dominate their particular arena with their personalities, people who completely own their success, people who cause others to approach *them* with multi-million or even multi-billion dollar deals, just because they know that having these superstars' names attached to a project or company will almost guarantee success.

When you become aware of these kinds of people and you're at just the right moment of your life, it's like being hit by a lightning bolt. And you think, "Whoa! This person is the ultimate. I want to be *exactly like them*."

For the first time, perhaps, you clearly see what you want your future to be – a future where, if you do what these super-successful people do, you end up with the same incredible opportunities and influence that they have.

And that's where it can get a little dangerous.

While it's awesome to be inspired by amazing achievers who have literally changed the face of the business world, there is a risk of becoming....well, *too* inspired.

To me, imitation is the highest form of flattery...and one of the biggest traps you can fall into.

THE SONG SHOULDN'T REMAIN THE SAME

There's a difference between emulating someone you want to be like – and just plain imitating them. In the first instance, you take their best qualities and adapt them to who *you* are. In the second instance, you actually try to do everything exactly the way they do it – even though you can't possibly do it as well as they do.

Because you are not them!

You see, there's a reason Elvis impersonators don't become known by their own names. Nobody wants them to be who *they* really are – no, their fans only want them to *pretend* to be Elvis. Of course, they could never actually be Elvis – they can only bring back great memories of The King of Rock N' Roll.

Elvis may have inspired these musicians to begin with. And these musicians undoubtedly have to have some talent to pull off a credible Elvis impersonation. But because they only present themselves as a *shadow* of someone famous, rather than developing their own unique personality, they're trapped. And if they ever want to become a singer that actually reflects their own personality, they usually have to start from scratch.

You can always enjoy an outright tribute act to a great performer. However, if they have the musical chops, they can bring back some awesome memories. But when you're perceived as ripping off a beloved icon, that's another story. And, since I am involved in the music business, I'd like to offer another musical example that illustrates just that scenario.

Anybody remember a rock band named "The Knack"? In 1979, their first album yielded a huge worldwide number one hit, "My Sharona," which you still hear played today. It didn't sound like anything else at the time – so you would think these guys had it made, right?

Wrong. The band itself ended up enraging rock fans and music critics at the time – because their first album cover art was a copy of the first Beatles' album – down to the band's haircuts. Now, if it had been some kind of clever 'spin' on the Beatles' album cover, they probably could have gotten away with it – but instead, it was almost a replica of the real deal. This resulted in a huge backlash that doomed their next effort and turned them into a footnote in rock history.

The sad fact is, it doesn't have to be that way. You can use the people who inspire you in a way that helps you succeed as an individual. Billy Joel has been a top act since 1973 – and there's a good reason for his singular success. In a recent interview, he talked about how he used his inspirations growing up. "I'm a product of what I heard while I was growing up," said Joel. "I synthesize my take on Ray Charles or the Beatles. That's where I'm coming from."

Note that he never made a point of singing his musical idols' songs. Or dressing up like them. Or duplicating their artwork. No, what he did was incorporate their techniques and their kind of showmanship into what *he* was doing – so he developed his own, strong personal identity that paid off for him. That's how he became an *authentic* musical success.

And by doing so, he avoided being trapped by the shadows of the greats – and he also avoided a huge backlash by not ripping off those legends either. Nobody thinks of Billy Joel as being anyone other than Billy Joel. And yet, the man openly admits liberally borrowing from the musical influences of his youth. By developing his own sound, however, and staying true to himself, he created his own indelible stamp that still resonates after three decades in the music business.

THE DAN KENNEDY TRAP

What works in the music business works in any business. Because it's still, ultimately, all about *business*. The best thing *any* business person can do is create their own strong, authentic personality that carries through their company's image and PR. You can always make a few bucks by slavishly imitating those more successful than you – but you can never truly earn respect or the profitability you desire, unless you create and develop your own individual template for achievement.

One of my big inspirations in the business world is master marketer Dan Kennedy. That's why I'm proud to be a business partner of his in Kennedy's All-American Barber Club® (www.KennedysBarberClub.com - if you're curious!) Now, if you know anything about Dan, you understand that he is a very *unique* personality. He drives professionally in about 100 harness races a year, purposely avoids and disparages slick-looking modern advertising, and is impossible to reach by phone. Yes, in the year 2010, the only way you can communicate with Dan Kennedy is… **by fax**.

In other words, he pretty much breaks every business rule there is in the world and makes it work for him - because he is very much his own person. And yes, I follow many of his precepts – but only in terms of what I *want* to project about myself, my business and my image. By absorbing his ideas through my own filter, I'm still Nick Nanton – and I don't end up being seen as Dan Kennedy Jr.. Trust me – I have zero interest in trying harness racing!

Many of the business people that I work with and I meet through what we affectionately call "Planet Dan" (this is the network of businesspeople who attend Dan's seminars, read his books and generally are fans of his teachings) - go through what I call *"the 4 Stages of Kennedy"*. I think this progression is incredibly similar to anyone else's who suddenly stumbles upon a personality that they desperately want to mimic in their professional life.

Stage 1 is simply... **"Dan Kennedy is insane!"** When someone first sees Dan's "No B.S.", punch-to-the-head style of copywriting, looks over Dan's rough, unpolished marketing materials and finds out that....wait, this guy only takes faxes???...., they immediately think Dan's a psycho, I'm a psycho for promoting Dan and everybody in our Glazer-Kennedy marketing group is drinking something they shouldn't be. But something lures them in...

....and then comes **Stage 2...**"Dan Kennedy is God!" The person suddenly understands how effective Dan's approaches are, how he's attracted all these followers with his incredible, instinctive marketing talents and how his methods can make money for any viable business. Their mind is completely blown and they have the burning fever of the recently-converted. And yes, now the convert seems like he's 'drinking the kool-aid' too!

That fever takes a long while to cool down, because **Stage 3** ends up being, **"I will BE Dan Kennedy!"** Instead of becoming an Elvis impersonator, the person decides to become a Dan Kennedy impersonator (one advantage is you don't need a sequined jumpsuit to be the latter). So he begins modeling his entire *modus operandi* on Dan's. Being only in touch by fax? Amazing idea! Telling people what to do and how to do it without pulling any punches? Outstanding! Hey, who knows where the best place is to learn harness racing?

And then brutal reality comes knocking on this guy's door. He realizes Dan Kennedy can get away with a lot of his quirks because he's been regarded as a marketing genius for decades; Dan's earned his "street cred", so he knows he can do as he 'darn well' pleases. Our Dan Kennedy newbie, on the other hand, is usually in the beginning steps of establishing himself and his business. He finds out he can't afford to solely use a fax machine instead of a cell phone, nor does he *really* want to. He actually *enjoys* communicating with customers, prospects...and even friends, on a regular basis!

(Oh, and he stinks at harness racing.)

So, if he's smart, he now progresses to **Stage 4 - "I'm just going to LEARN everything I can from Dan Kennedy."** That means personally adapting and integrating Dan's rules and techniques – but still remaining *who you are*.

Just as Billy Joel integrated the work of the greats who inspired him into his own authentic music, our new Dan Kennedy disciple has learned to likewise funnel the Dan Kennedy marketing magic through his own filter. And nobody looks down on him as if he's just a pale copy of the real Dan Kennedy.

MAKE YOUR OWN KIND OF MUSIC

Obviously, **Stage 4** is what you want to shoot for whenever an impressive person inspires you. But how do you avoid merely imitating the greats – when what you should be doing is integrating what they have to offer into your own persona?

First and foremost, you have to figure out who *you* are and *what you want*. You, your personality and your passions are the foundation for your growth and development, both as a human being and as a business person. "To thine own self be true," goes the Shakespearean maxim and that still holds true 500 years later. I won't be around in another 500 years, unless science has some *really* amazing breakthroughs, but I expect that thought will still be quoted then.

Second, break down what works for you and what doesn't; where you need either a complete change of direction or where you just need to make adjustments to improve your results. To realize your ambitions, this is essential.

Finally, decide how to add needed value to who you are and what you do. This is where you should search for the proper coaches, mentors and role models who have already achieved what you want to achieve. Analyze *how* they made that magic happen – then see how their different methodologies apply to what you do, how you do it and the areas where you need to make adjustments.

The big lesson here? *Never try to play someone else's game. Instead, fit theirs into your own.*

That's how I help my clients achieve celebrity status in their fields. Obviously, they have to offer something different to stand out – and, to properly brand them, we employ proven strategies used by some of the most successful business people of all time. But we use those strategies to *support* and *promote* who our clients are, not to make them into something they're not.

When you integrate instead of imitate, you eliminate a lot of self-imposed limitations and open up a world of possibilities. So don't be an Elvis impersonator. It's always better to be your own King...and *that's* how you can *ignite your business and transform your world,* as well as the worlds of so many more people who you'll now be able to help – because they see you as the real deal, not merely an impersonator.

ABOUT NICK

Nick Nanton, Esq. is known as "The Celebrity Lawyer" for his role in developing and marketing business and professional experts into Celebrity Experts in their field, through personal branding, to help them gain credibility and recognition for their accomplishments. Nick is recognized as the nation's leading expert on personal branding as Fast Company Magazine's Expert Blogger on the subject and lectures regularly on the topic at the University of Central Florida. His book Celebrity Branding You® has been selected as the textbook on personal branding at the University.

Nick serves as the Producer of America's Premier Experts® television show and The Next Big Thing® radio show, both designed to recognize the top Experts in their field and bring their solutions to consumers.

Nick is an award-winning songwriter and television producer and has worked on everything from large scale events to 'reality tv' pitches with the likes of Bill Cosby, President George H.W. Bush, Superbowl Champion Don Shula, Legendary Basketball Coach Bobby Knight, Rock 'n Roll Hall of Famer, Stan Lynch (Tom Petty & The Heartbreakers) and many more. Nick is recognized as one of the top thought leaders in the business world and has co-authored the best-selling books, Celebrity Branding You!®, Big Ideas for Your Business, Shift Happens and Power Principles for Success and has interviewed some of the top business leaders in the world, including Donald Trump (The Trump Organization), Richard Branson (Virgin Group) and Tony Hsieh (Zappos.com). Nick also serves as editor and publisher of Celebrity Press™, a publishing company that produces and releases books by top Business Experts. CelebrityPress has published books by Brian Tracy, Mari Smith, Ron LeGrand and many other celebrity experts. He has also published books for more than 60 best-selling authors. Nick has been featured in USA Today, The Wall St. Journal, Newsweek, The New York Times, Entrepreneur® Magazine, FastCompany.com and has appeared on ABC, NBC, CBS, and FOX television affiliates speaking on subjects ranging from branding, marketing and law, to American Idol.

Nick is a member of the Florida Bar, holds a JD from the University of

Florida Levin College of Law, as well as a BSBA in Finance from the University of Florida's prestigious Warrington College of Business. Nick is a voting member of The National Academy of Recording Arts & Sciences (NARAS, Home to The GRAMMYs), a 4-time Telly Award winner, and spends his spare time working with Young Life, Florida Hospital and rooting for the Florida Gators with his wife Kristina, and their two sons, Brock and Bowen.

To connect with Nick:

800-980-1626
Nick@CelebrityBrandingAgency.com
Twitter.com/NickNanton
Facebook.com/NickNanton

CHAPTER 13

LIFESTYLE OF THE RICH AND CONSCIOUS – RECYCLE YOUR HUMAN POTENTIAL

BY DARSANA ROLDAN

When I was first invited to co-author this book, I was in the middle of getting ready to take my first nationwide tour in our luxury RV with my best friend and wife, Kalyani, our two precious young children, Jivani and Jamaili, and our eight amazing animal babies, teaching others to Recycle Their Human Potential. Not only that, but I was in the final weeks of a three month winter vacation in the Sierra Nevada Mountains nurturing my inner growth while having a lot of fun with my family...The point is that although it may seem to others that I could have said no, I knew immediately that I had to recycle my reactions and say YES to Life!

The reason I mention this is because this is the first thing I want to bring to your awareness! In all honesty, regardless of who you are, if you are not willing to open yourself to what life has to offer and to take risks in life, this chapter is not for you!

Think about it... Life Itself is *our MOST precious gift EVER*! Everything that you have ever experienced and will ever experience is because you are ALIVE! And the truth is that all of us only have a certain amount of time to make the best of it. So you would think that most people would be having a blast everyday and only doing things that support them being happy, fulfilled and prosperous; but they are not! Not me. As Nelson Mandela suggested, I always want to become greater than I already am. How far am I willing to go to figure out how to transcend any situation that could be sabotaging my life? I would rather die than quit because I don't know how to settle for mediocrity... seriously!

Am I grateful? Absolutely. I live my life in complete gratitude; as a matter of fact, gratitude is a tremendous force as to why I have the quality of life that I have now. But I also know that not living my full potential doesn't serve me or my family well, and stops me from experiencing all the amazing things that I am doing in this world! For that reason, I am always 'reaching for the stars'. Just a couple of years ago, I walked away from the 'success' that many people dream of, but I knew I had to do it to be where I am now. Why? Because nothing is more fulfilling to me than to know that I am teaching my children through my own example to go after their dreams! If I die today, I will be completely satisfied with my life. I can look myself and them straight in the eyes and say, "I consistently walk my talk and therefore I have no regrets." My question to you is... can you say the same?

You see I spent the first 27 years of my life trying to get ahead, but always feeling like I was behind. Going through the journey of overcoming alcoholism and drug addiction over 21 years ago changed my interpretation of what adversities represent and pushed me into Recycling My Human Potential. Through that initial journey, I realized that I can transcend any challenge or adversity and use it to co-create anything I believe in.

Do I know that I am responsible for everything that happens in my life? Absolutely! But that doesn't mean that I have it all figured out to the point that I don't face situations of challenge and adversity! It means that I have mastered my mental faculties so when the day-to-day situations show up, big or small, I see them for what they are - opportunities to Recycle My Human Potential and deliver the results I want. Am I setting the intention to attract more challenges? Of course not, but believe me there will be plenty coming my way anyway as long as I am alive! How else can I grow and evolve?

I believe that no matter how much money you have, how healthy you are, or how evolved you perceive yourself to be, life continues to bring along many challenges. This is 'no big deal' once you **understand the purpose behind it**! Why? Because although this is where MOST people give up their ability to manifest their dreams, at the same time this is where the answer to their problems exists. How important is this? Extremely important, because it means that with some guidance, most people can transform their lives in a very short amount of time! You see, 'True Success' is a lifestyle and once you learn how to Recycle Your Human Potential, everything has value in it, especially the things that you don't like.

Even if you had all the money in the world, if you don't live a healthy life, it is all over. You can also be 'happy as a clown', but if you don't reveal the ability to manifest money, you are limited in the things you can do for yourself, your family and the world. There are many components to having an extraordinary life. So why not have it all? I hear many people talk about how successful they are, but if you ask their loved ones what they think, you will be surprised to hear their feedback (especially if you ask their children or significant others).

What I have experienced myself, and with thousands of clients, is that we give up the power to manifest our dreams, because we are engaging in a lifestyle that drains our resources within. I mean this literally. It is exhausting and life-consuming to live that way. Do you know the amount of energy that it takes to look at yourself in the mirror and not like what you see? Or how about spending over 2,500 hours a year doing something that doesn't bring you fulfillment? Imagine what it takes to always be worrying about not having enough, competing for more, or stressed out about your finances. If that doesn't 'drain the hell out of you', I don't know what does! And the killer one for me... how much energy it takes to justify to yourself when you know that you are teaching your children that mediocracy is completely acceptable? I don't know about you, but I'm committed to being extraordinary and I can guarantee you that my children know this!

Whether you are dealing with addictions, procrastination, self-sabotage, self conditioning, compulsive behaviors, constant fear, or you name it, I want to share with you this powerful and dynamic approach to life. If you want to *Ignite Your Business* and *Change The World,* you MUST overcome these issues FIRST! Is this journey easy? Honestly, it's different for everyone. I personally, constantly and consciously *participate in the co-creation of my life.* That's just me. And since I know that I am doing my part, I have an *expectancy* of always attracting everything I need for the manifestation of my heart's desires. So when opportunities show up, I *take risks* because I understand and trust the process. David Neagle, said, "Faith is not a jump in the dark, it is a walk in the light. Faith is not guessing, it's knowing something."

Since there are no limits when it comes to happiness, fulfillment and prosperity, wherever you are in your life, there is room to grow. For that reason, when you are feeling frustrated, scared, alone, rejected, disappointed, angry, victimized or whatever, right then is the time to dissolve the power that it has over you by bringing TRUTH into your consciousness. The carpenter from Galilee said, "You are the light of the World" and he meant what he said. On the other hand, if you choose NOT to recycle it, you have once again given your inner power away, created a bigger destructive mental pattern, attached a negative emotion to it and requested another similar or worse experience to come your way in the near future, because you didn't do what your individual Soul was leading you to do; to set yourself FREE and become whole again from the inside out!

It is extremely important that whenever something comes up, you make a commitment to recycle it as soon as possible, otherwise you will talk yourself out of doing it later. The deletion filters in your mind will do what they know how to do best; justify, make excuses, blame, judge, confirm your old story and any other creative way you may have developed throughout the years, to avoid taking responsibility! I don't mean to sound harsh, but remember what I told you at the beginning. Life is too precious to waste any moment of it!

In order to bring clarity to the Recycling Process, let's highlight the understanding that everything is energy and that energy flows where attention goes. In his book, *The Science Of Getting Rich*, author Wallace D. Wattles talks about the Law of Perpetual Transmutation. "Energy from the formless realm is constantly flowing into the material world and taking form. This energy is limitless and inexhaustible. As old forms are exhausted, they give way to new forms that emerge from the invisible hidden energy of the universe."

We all know the tremendous impact that our upbringing, conditioning, perceptions and interpretations, have on our ability to give form to our individual reality. In another words we seem to be co-creating experiences that keep us connected with our childhood. The biggest challenge is probably not so much what we know consciously, but what we use sub-consciously to give form to our current reality. Leo Buscaglia said, "The easiest thing to do is to be yourself." Unfortunately, that is not what most of us were taught to do. Beware, that although it is essential that you do the work to claim your authenticity and uniqueness, it is as important not to get caught up in the drama of releasing the past. Remember energy flows where attention goes. The Recycling Process is a dynamic way of experiencing life completely different to what you and I have been exposed and conditioned to believe in. But the demand is here now, because we are all looking to find a way to have **richer life**...

RE-EVALUATE This is about 'putting your money where your mouth is'... no pun intended. While forgiving yourself and everyone involved for whatever happened up to this point, from now on you are going to take ownership of what's really important to YOU! Accepting that wherever you are is where you need to start, will lead you as you re-evaluate your priorities throughout every situation. Here is where you 'dig deep into your Soul' and give new form to the Divine energy flowing through you, because you realize that you are NOT YOUR STORY. This is where you *love* yourself enough to take full responsibility for everything. I mean everything! Every choice and decision you make from now on is based on the pre-determined commitment to Recycle Your Human Potential! You will be amazed about your ability to transcend challenges and situations that used to get the best of you, because you are now activating and releasing the power within the REAL YOU!

REMIND is about remembering the intuition you came with into this world. For the most part we were all forced to abandon our sense of Oneness from the moment we were born. *NO! YOU CAN'T DO THAT! WAIT! STOP!* and many other words and indications that created for us the illusion of separation as babies. This step is to remind you that 'what the mind can conceive, it can achieve', because you were created in the full image of whatever you believe created you. And of course I am NOT talking about your parents. You must **remind** yourself of the feelings and experiences that can re-establish your confidence and your willingness to face anything that comes your way because you realize that there is a guarantee of laws acting upon your beliefs! You must hold on to the memories that build up your self-esteem and use your mental faculties to allow you to see the next step in your journey of *Self* discovery. Calming your finite mind through practices like meditation allows the Infinite Mind to flow through you as you, because you are an individualized center of all that is GOOD!

The cool thing is that although you have to do it yourself, you don't have to do it alone. Take full advantage to learn from other individuals that obviously are 'walking their talk'. You will gain tremendous confidence every time you recycle a challenge and shortly you will have enough memories 'to move a mountain'.

RECONNECT is absolutely the most important because it is about feeling and being *self secure by consciously reconnecting with yourself, others, nature, animals and the planet*. I also believe this is where most people are losing their greatest ability to bring their visions into fruition! Regardless of your religious or scientific beliefs about life, there are obvious Universal Laws and Principles that govern everything from our bodies to the solar system. Since you and I are part of this infinite interconnected Creation, everything matters. From our thoughts, feelings, actions, beliefs, choices, relationships, conversations, the food we eat, how we give back, our gratitude and many other components of our lifestyle.

As you Recycle Your Human Potential you will continue to reveal your own answers about happiness, fulfillment and prosperity! You will intuitively align yourself with the most powerful forces and resources you need to manifest your dreams! You will continue to develop greater awareness and you will realize that you can't miss what you haven't experienced before. Learning from other individuals will no longer be a threat and investing in yourself will become your number one priority. I can go on and on about how magnificent life can be, but that doesn't really matter right now because you have to find that out for yourself. So take this book and make it a turning point by taking immediate action. As I said in the beginning, *our MOST precious gift EVER is LIFE!*

I believe that if you are reading this book, it is because you are one of the individuals who are shifting the Consciousness of our world. The Lifestyle of The Rich and Conscious Movement is a massive group of people internationally who LOVE humanity, animals and the planet, and who USE money to live extraordinary lives. Our main objective and the reason why I co-authored this book is to stir up the gift of Truth within each one of us so that we may celebrate living to our fullest potential. Ernest Holmes said, "Many will hear, but only a few will listen." My final question to you is... Are you Loving, Giving and Willing to say YES to life NOW?

ABOUT DARSANA

Darsana Roldan is a conscious, life visionary with a passion for living in freedom and abundance. Humor and truth are his authentic way of assisting clients to Recycle Their Human Potential. He is also co-creator of the revolutionary Lifestyle of the Rich and Conscious Movement of Real People Living Extraordinary Lives.

Through his personal journey of completely releasing alcohol and drug addiction over 21 years ago, Darsana recycled his interpretation of what challenges and adversities represent to break free from the prison of the mind. For the past 16 years, Darsana has been immersed in studying and growing in every aspect of physical, emotional, intellectual and spiritual wealth and prosperity with many of the most profound teachers in the world.

Darsana's giving has immersed him in a colorful array of exciting experiences of organizing and leading youth camps and programs, founding the Conscious Kingdom no kill animal sanctuary, and founding and developing one of the most prominently effective educational agencies, providing both Spanish and English clientele strategies for Positive Parenting and release of Drugs, Alcohol, and Domestic Violence. As well as creating and expanding two successful bilingual/bicultural real estate companies.

With his unending commitment to living in harmony and alignment with more life for all humanity, animals, nature, and the planet, Darsana lives a richly abundant and fulfilling life centered in spiritual principles, playful parenting and prosperity consciousness and it is his purpose and passion to dissolve the illusion of separation by bringing TRUTH to the minds of millions for One Love, One Wealth, One World!

With their uniquely fun approach to life, Darsana with his wife and soul partner, Kalyani, currently travel the country, with their two young children and eight animals, in their Luxury RV, magnetizing people of all ages, with their essential roadmap for freedom, money, and meaning.

While sharing the same strategies they have used to embrace adversities and challenges, by recycling them into powerful turning points, they have empowered thousands of clients to uplevel their lifestyle choices and financial prosperity, and reconnect with what's meaningful to them.

Kalyani and Darsana have fully stepped out to celebrate life! It is their truest purpose and passion in life to spread their energy of soulful love teaching people how to live on purpose, achieving extraordinary levels of true fulfillment, wealth, and freedom while giving back a profoundly positive impact on the world, resulting in a more globally sustainable and compassionate humanity.

To revolutionize your life or your event with Kalyani and Darsana Roldan, please contact (877) SEEK-TO-GROW, or (877) 733-5864 and visit www. LifestyleoftheRichandConscious.com